Silvia Sutherland
Thank you!

GET UP

SILVIA SUTHERLAND

Copyright © 2012 SILVIA SUTHERLAND

All rights reserved.

ISBN:9798866899227

DEDICATION

To my children, my sisters and all the other angels.

ACKNOWLEDGMENTS

Rachel from 100% proofreading , I could not have done this without you.
My daughter for your patience and brilliance.

FORWARD

If you know me personally this book will contain information about me you probably did not previously know. It may be upsetting for you to read so do proceed with caution. This book started out as a way to release the pain and trauma I had experienced or indeed was going through at the time. It has evolved into a piece of work that I have chosen to share because of the lessons I have learned, the discoveries I have made and its relevance to my work as a therapist. This is a book about my life. To use a word I rarely agree with, it would be impossible for me to write a book about myself without including members of my family and other people that I have met, who have influenced my life in some way. I fully accept that my perspective upon events in my life, that includes any of these people, will be entirely different to everyone else's perspective. I have viewed them through my personal filter system. I also fully accept that the people I mention in the book may completely disagree with my perspective or version of events. They will have quite rightly viewed the events through their own personal filter system. I have included events in this book that involve other people to illustrate and explain my story, not anyone else's story. No events were added for sensationalism. I am grateful for each and every person and the lessons they brought and still bring to what we call the great tapestry of life.

CHAPTER 1

On the face of it I had a big, nice house, money in the bank, a good job and a sensible, reliable husband who didn't hit me if I spoke out of line. My children had food and clothes and resources to thrive. When you hear the beginning of this story you could easily have said that, at this point, I had recovered and made it. Life was now good, a success and safe, yes? But this was not the case. One big lesson here. Big houses and money do not bring safety and happiness, in fact they make the sadness even more distressing.

"You should be happy now, what more do you want?"

I felt like an outsider, observing myself. I now understand this as dissociation, a thing that happens to our minds when reality is just too difficult. It's protection and our brains love to protect. So, as if I wasn't really there, I watched this 40-year-old woman and her child and observed what was going on.

The mother was on the settee, and she looked tired, tired beyond belief. She was motionless, and her five-year-old child, in sharp contrast, was a flurry of activity. The little child was talking, screaming and moving, and her face was telling this mother that she was distressed, that she was desperate for her mother to respond in some way. The mother still wasn't moving. Her eyes were open though, and she was looking. She was really looking, and she was really thinking. She was thinking that this emotional disaster facing her was a true reflection of how she felt right now, and she somehow envied the small child and their ability to express themselves so freely. She was thinking that had she not felt so paralysed with tiredness this was exactly how she felt like behaving. Inside her she was screaming. It was so loud, and it was so strong, and it made her feel quite unwell to have all of this noise inside her body, inside her head. But as this observation embedded itself in her mind, the mother began to move. Slowly but surely, the pain in her child's eyes twisted and turned and seeped its way into her conscious mind, and the mother remembered. It felt a long way back and hard to see, but it was a memory, true enough. She was the mother. She dug down deep inside, and she pulled, and she pushed, and she heaved her head out of the deep fog surrounding her and she moved ever so slowly towards her child. She held her furious child, and she felt the sorriest she had ever felt for anything in her life. This helpless child needed her mother, and she was the only mother this child had. She remembered that being a mother was a job she was once good at, and her child needed her to get up. Get up! **Get Up!**

CHAPTER TWO

The year of my 40th birthday is when all of this really started. And by 'this' I mean getting to a place in my life where I can find peace. It was a harsh discovery – which is often the way when you hit a significant milestone in your life – that my life so far had been filled with a lot of tough times and sadness. A lot of my life had been ruined by this feeling. I don't mean that I never had good times, because I did, just not very many when I looked back. That in itself made me feel regretful for a good while, which added itself on top of all the other negative feelings in my body.

'Life begins at 40,' they say.

Even the idea of this filled me with dread. The first 40 years had been exhausting so the thought of doing it all again seemed unimaginable. I felt like 40 years was just the right amount of life, and if I could choose then I would be saying, I'm 40 and I've had enough life thank you very much.

Life is often referred to as a rollercoaster. Full of ups and downs. I thought, if life really is a roller coaster, then it should therefore be acceptable to get off when you have had enough. It wouldn't matter if you were 40 or not, you could just wave to the young lad in the little cabin operating the ride, give him the nod and he would stop the ride and let you off. You could wander off and have a cup of tea somewhere, perhaps a fairground doughnut, in peace, away from all the ups and downs. All the people left on board would have chosen to stay so they would be happy. You could see them all merrily waving at you as you enjoyed a well-earned rest. Unfortunately, getting off the ride of life was not an option, so as always life had carried on, as had I. Circumstances forced me to think, if I really did have to do it all again, could I make it any better? Could I recover from all the sadness? Looking back on how much of a struggle life has been, I might have chosen to get off, as it were, but I did not, and this is my story. The story that takes me to today, aged 46, feeling, well… *feeling*. That is a good start.

CHAPTER THREE

Berwick granny judged people on how clever and how attractive they were. It was quite harsh to say the least, but that's what she did, and everyone was placed into a category accordingly. Clever, but not a looker, that was one category. A looker but not very clever, that was another. Either of these categories were acceptable, and of course if you were clever and a looker, well, you were top of the class in her books. If you were neither clever nor handsome then unfortunately you were quite low down the pecking order, but you could redeem yourself if you were extraordinarily kind and hardworking. She didn't mean any harm, in fact, despite her harsh tongue at times, she was one of the kindest and most generous people in the world. I remember sitting with her once watching the news. A woman had lost all her belongings in a house fire and was by herself with her children, with nowhere to go. My granny wondered how she could find this woman and let her and her children come and stay with her and at the very least she tried to find out how she could get some money to her. This was typical of her and the way she opened her heart to anyone who needed it. This, of course, was before the internet was used to do this kind of thing with a mere click of a button.

As I matured, I understood that my grandmother was very unfair on herself and lacked the confidence that I would have awarded her if I could. Berwick Granny would say to me as a child,

> "I used to have a nice face before I got old."

I had looked at her and I saw an old face yes, but a kind face and a safe face. Women are so harsh on themselves. Social media didn't exist in my grandmother's day, but it did not stop the berating of the image of the female. Unrealistic images of women and the persecution of females in whatever form that has taken, has been the work of men over centuries. Threatened by the attributes of women, men have shut us down. The world didn't start out like that, but that is how it has become. The time I have wasted looking at my own face wishing it was different, wishing it was prettier, wishing it was thinner, fatter, less spotty, more tanned, on and on and on I have gone, battering myself for years, when all the time it has been my very own face.

I would put Berwick Granny in the clever, kind, beautiful, and hardworking category. I miss her terribly, and it breaks my heart that my own children didn't have her in their lives for long, and my youngest not at all. Along with granny and my mother, there were so many others in my life who never got to see their lovely faces. Berwick Granny lived a long life, she was matriarch of the family and when she passed away at the grand old age of 91, I do hope that she had enjoyed her life, and that she knew she was loved.

I loved to listen to granny talk about my mother. So very few people in my life knew my mother, so it was difficult to keep her memories alive. My mother died when I was 15 years old. I really only knew her for such a tiny part of my life in retrospect, but what an impact that woman made upon me.

Brigid, my mother, was the second oldest in the family. She had an older brother and two younger siblings, a girl and a boy. Brigid had fitted into the beautiful and clever category. Not quite as clever as her older brother but extremely clever none the less. This was a good start for her, and added to this Brigid was a good person, a hardworking person and a person that everybody liked. It was all going so well. She moved to Edinburgh to study art when she finished school, and this was all very cool and wacky and, coming from a small town like Berwick, I am sure was exactly what my mother had been craving. Nonetheless, she had lived her early life in such a small place that I am quite sure that as an 18-year-old woman she was fairly naïve. As strong as she was when I knew her, I could imagine that her head would be easily turned by a seemingly exotic man with long hair, whose father was an architect and lived in a *castle*, no less, in the highlands of Scotland. And this is what happened. My mother became involved with this curious man, and really that was the start of the end of her longed-for future as an artist, for before long she became pregnant with her first child, my big sister, Jane. This was in a period when people were expected to get married if they were having a baby together, and also an era where being a wife was a role that didn't very often allow you to have a career as well. After all, the guilt that is still evident today in working mothers was not founded on myth and legend. Centuries of ongoing persecution of the feminine spirt has kept women in cages and this conditioning and trauma is carried through our bodies, through our DNA, on and on until we set about changing it. It is slowly changing, but these ancestral chains are heavy, and we have had to work hard; we still have to work hard, to break free of them.

So, my mother married this long-haired man, who jetted off

to Spain on a whim to buy a guitar, who held wild celebrity-filled parties, and who was right smack-bang in the middle of the groovy LSD and marijuana-smoking days. When it was cool, you know, not like now when it causes serious mental health disorders and death. I am not anti-cannabis, or indeed LSD, because of the understanding I now have about the immense benefits of these plants and others that come from our beloved mother Gia. The issue I have is the criminalisation and subsequent corruption and exploitation of these substances designed to manipulate the vulnerable who are then the ones at risk of serious mental health disorders and death with no societal support. But in the 60s and 70s it was groovy, and what's not fun about all of that?

Brigid was stuffed back into a cage after her brief brush with freedom, and three more children were born. She and her husband lived in the castle in the highlands for a period, but then moved into a cottage on the grounds, which sounds, I am sure, like a simply spiffing fairy-tale life. In reality—because let's face it, this is not a fairy tale—the cottage was cold, rundown, and full of damp, and as her husband did not in fact have an actual job, after all his partying, and grooving about, the family had very little money to live on. A woman in those times would have genuinely expected her husband to provide for her, and while my mother had the ability to get a job, and could have gone to work, there was no one to look after the children and the father would simply not have been expected to do that. I think of my mother in this place, and I feel so sorry for her. Sitting alone with children takes you to one of the loneliest places on earth. She left home with everything at her fingertips, including beauty, and perhaps she thought she had got it all when she found this man and had these children, but I suspect she definitely had not. All my own personal memories and experiences of my mother told me that she was a mother first and foremost. She may have been many things, but as a child I was never in any doubt that my mother could be and would be my biggest champion. This mostly came into play when I was at risk, or she was at risk of anybody seeing any kind of weakness in her. She could be terrifying. She would not back down if she felt she was right or if there was any kind of injustice going on. Somewhere along the line, though, she wasn't getting what she needed or wanted, and she found herself with these four children, all under the age of five, away from her family. This must have been hard because she would have fought tooth and nail for another woman in this position who needed any sort of help. I suppose she must have inherited this from my granny. Probably because she had few other people in her life, she would talk to me quite a lot about this time and about her husband. One story has always stuck in my mind, probably because she told it so well and probably because it was so shocking to me as a young child. It was the time that he had come home for tea with one of his friends having taken one of those groovy LSD tabs.

"They were giggling away like school kids at the table, I was furious!" My mother had told me.

I imagine the scene right now. A table in the living area of the damp rundown cottage, not one item of furniture fitting with the other and a mismatch of plates on the table. The four young girls sitting on their chairs and the two fully grown men among them, unaware of their presence, unaware of how these children were perceiving them and this situation. My mother ladling out the spaghetti onto their plates, gently for the children, with more force and fury for the giggling men. No doubt my mother had spent the day alone entertaining the children, cooking this meal which was not being appreciated, and missing out on the fun and antics they had been up to that afternoon.

As unbelievable as it sounds today with our vast awareness

of mental illness, my mother never believed him to be as unwell as he was. Today, despite the atrocious lack of mental health care in the NHS at least, he was so unwell that he would have been helped, but they were isolated and unfamiliar with his condition, and he received no help from anyone that really could have made a difference.

The youngest child at the time, Kay, was a baby in arms when he died. My mother told me, that she was down in the cottage, and she heard a gunshot. She told me that she ran to the castle, up to one of the high rooms and she found her husband dead. Understandably, I was taken aback by this tale, and my graphic imagination was working overtime as she spoke. Inside I wondered why she had decided to share this information, but I didn't voice my thoughts. If she told me this now, I would have many more questions. Where were my sisters at the time, the baby in arms? How did she know which room to go to? What did she do? Did she try to revive him, or was it such a gruesome sight that she knew that wasn't an option? I will never know; these are unanswered questions that will remain so.

My mother told me this story one day when, ironically, she was also dying, although I was unaware of this fact at the time. She was in bed, as was the norm at the time, and she was sitting talking with me while I sat on the edge. I used to go and see her and sit and chat. I would always try and get her to get out of bed. I knew deep down she couldn't, and perhaps I wanted to make her feel guilty. I think I hoped that the guilt would get to her, and she would get up to overcome it. It was a bit of a test. Nothing had stopped her looking after me before so what was different this time? How could I get back the familiarity of having a mother who wasn't in bed all day and looked after me in the same way as she had before?

What really struck me about this conversation on the bed that day was how much my mother cared for this man, when she spoke of him her love for him oozed with every word. She spoke like the lovestruck teenager she had been when they met, those intense feelings so beautifully and tragically suspended in time. She shared with me how much she still missed him. Even after the LSD at the dinner table? Well, ok.

My mother told me that after he died, she remembered something she had been told or had read about astral travel. She thought she would give it a go and she would try and visit this man who she missed so much. She said that she lay in her room at the cottage, and she thought about floating out of her body, and to her surprise she found that it worked. She had floated out of her body and out through the window, and into the trees.

"What was it like?" I asked, astonished.

"It was lovely" my mother told me, and her eyes looked off into the distance past me as she remembered.

"It was like flying, and I spun around the branches of the trees for a while and I wondered if I could stay there forever, it felt so nice. But I did go back," she said, "and I didn't find who I was looking for."

CHAPTER FOUR

When I knew, and I mean actually knew, I was unwell, I went to the doctor and told her. That is all I knew to do. For years before that I had stumbled in and out of depression. Sometimes I took medication, and it eased it for a while, and sometimes I could shake it off myself, but this time I was simply too tired. It felt to me that the effort now of moving my body, of standing up, of speaking even, was so immense that I could no longer bear it. I felt small. As tiny and small as I had ever felt in my life. It was as if I had started off my life wearing a coat. The coat was light, and it kept me warm and dry, and I could jump and run and play in this coat. Each time I had suffered it was like a shower of rain down on me and my coat. At first it was easy to run around and dry off the wet, but as the showers fell faster and heavier it became increasingly hard to dry off before the next downpour fell and the coat got heavier and heavier, and I became helpless under its weight. I felt at that point that the coat was so sodden that it had lost all shape and usefulness. The sleeves hung down way past my hands, restricting their use. I liked to pull the hood up over my head now and hide under the dripping ledge. It was weighted with sorrow, but I could hide deep down inside it unnoticed. I didn't want to be seen, I wanted to hide. It was hard living inside this dirty soaking mess, but it deflected people, and that made me safe. I had to decide, however, if it was better to be safe or better to be happy, or was I able to have both? That day, as my child looked at me with such desperation, I had begun to move a little inside the coat, and I had lifted my arms and I had pushed my hands out of the sleeves just a small way. I had moved the hood so that I could peek through.

"Can you remember the first time you felt like this?" the counsellor asked me.

I could remember, yes, quite clearly as it happened. It was when I was 10 years old, and I moved with my mother and two of my sisters away from my home to a place where I was unsafe. This major life event has influenced so many decisions that I have made for my own children, to their detriment at times, that I cannot impress upon you enough the impact this one single life event had upon me and my life. The impact of one single event, one day, can change the course of everything.

After Brigid's husband died, she had continued to live in the cottage but by all accounts, that continued to be an unhappy existence for them all, and as Brigid was so desperately heartbroken this must have made for an extra element of distress, on top of the isolation, the lack of money, the lack of stimulation, the lack of family support, and the large number of children to look after. A grim picture. Her husband's father, my sister's Grandad, was a wealthy man and he knew wealthy people, or people who were in those circles, though being middle or upper class did not always mean you had money, as I have discovered in later life. One of these men had been a man by the name of Graham Sutherland. Graham was a farm owner, and he was from a family of great wealth who in their time owned many acres of land and property. There had been three brothers in total. My father would tell me tales of his uncles but as I write now, I don't recall any of them with certainty. I have a vague recollection of an uncle who had a hotel that served coloured mashed potato that they coloured with food dye. Did that really happen? What I do know is that some skulduggery went on and a lot of that famous Sutherland estate was lost.

Graham was friends with royalty, and walked in their circles too, demonstrating his knowledge of the mountains and the rocks and minerals they contained, and I even have photos of him sitting on the hills with prince, now King Charles. King Charles wrote to my father when Graham had died to give his condolences, I have the letter, which my father kept in a frame, to this day. The thing about Graham was that he also made up a lot of tales. A fantasist you might say. My mother saw right through him.

Graham Sutherland had two sons and a daughter and the youngest of these sons, William was somehow introduced to Brigid, and that was how my parents first met. William ran the Farm which was not far from their cottage. He lived there with his mother Katherine and on occasion Graham, I'll come to that part later. My mother had become pregnant with me and, as it was in those days, William and Brigid had to get married. My father, who could be extremely unkind with his words and actions, made no secret of the fact that he would not have ideally chosen to be in a relationship with a woman who already had four children, and I often thought that the way he talked made it seem as though wanted some sort of compensation. A story my mother told many times, and I can still hear as clear as day in my head is this:

"I said to your dad, if we haven't moved into the farm by the time the baby is 1 year old then we aren't coming. Do you know we moved in the day before your first birthday?"

My father was clear. He did not have the space for this

woman and all of her children. He had to build onto the end of the house to give them room. These times were so very different. I mean, could you imagine in this day and age, a woman getting pregnant to a man, and first of all having to marry him, and then could you imagine the woman's only option was to rely on him to now care for and provide for them all financially? Talk about prison walls. But, you know, if we look past the logistics of this, whatever they may be for each situation, shouldn't it be the case? Shouldn't it be the case that a man you love and who loves you back would support you and your children in any way that was needed? Not in my experience, but in relationships where people love each other they do want to support each other and any children that come along with that. My experiences in life have made me so incredibly desperate to rely upon absolutely no one. Although I have done a great amount of work on this particular issue, the deep-rooted beliefs remain somewhat. If you let someone help you, they will want a repayment. In my mother's case she had to deal with my father's resentment of the situation and her children, which was her payback for receiving his support. If you let someone help you, you may begin to rely upon them and where will that leave you when they disappear from your life? If you let someone help you, what does that say about you? You are weak and helpless, that's what it says, and when people think you are weak, they try to break you and to abuse you. These beliefs have taken years to form and years to break apart.

Spoiler alert, we did all move to the farm. The farm where my father had lived with his mother almost his whole life. The older brother and the younger sister had moved away, or should I say, escaped as soon as they could. Graham Sutherland had not been a kind father or a kind husband, but karma, well that really did catch up with him in later life.

CHAPTER FIVE

My father built a two-story extension onto the end of the original farmhouse. It had its own front door so as you went in there was an area where you could hang your coats and dump your wellies. Facing you was a little room which was used for many things but initially it was a larder with little shelves and cupboards which were filled with homemade jam and marmalade. My father owned a shotgun, which he used for shooting rabbits and occasionally deer, but that was only when necessary. He was a man who was in tune with nature and the very nature of being a farmer where you do need to kill your animals to make money to live made him appear unfeeling, but he did care and understand his animals and he would not wish any living creature harm if he could avoid it. It is very fashionable at the moment to connect ourselves with nature by taking the occasional forest bath, but this man was part of the land, he merged seamlessly with the ground.

My mother had been in charge of home décor and the whole place was decorated in Laura Ashley wallpaper. I can see the print now in my mind, and the colours. Cream background with pink flowers, and in one room yellow stripes with orange flowers dotted alongside them. I remember too all the little touches my mother had made in the house to make it her own. The seashells in the little bit of border she had dug around the front of the house. She had planted foxgloves and used the shells as the edging. Along the shelves where the jam sat, she had pinned on lace, and the jars had pretty labels which she had designed and glued on. A door on your left went into the living room. The room was small, and a person-wide archway went through to the kitchen. In the living room there was a wood-burning stove, which was the only heat source in the house, so in the winter this room was where everyone sat. Squeezed into the small space was a table surrounded by wooden chairs and a sofa. Next to the fire an Orkney chair sat, which was pretty uncomfortable, and in the corner was a piano. On the wall there were some shelves where the record player lived and, when I was older, a portable tv. The floor was stone and, although there was a rug on the floor, it was cold and uncomfortable. Oh, the heavenly luxury I experienced when I visited Berwick Granny who had fitted carpets in every room, even the stairs. You could walk in your bare feet and lie on the sitting room floor, and it felt so nice to relax there in this cosy warm environment. The farm was not cosy and while in the winter the sitting room was warm, the rest of the house was so cold it felt sometimes as though you never really warmed up. Going up to bed in the evening, we would line up as my mother would fill our hot water bottles. They were burning hot, but you were so cold you held them tightly onto your body as you left the warmth and went out to the stairs. The stairs were wooden and lead up to the bedrooms. At the top of the stairs to the right was my parents' room. When we very first got a TV there was some sort of mistake with the ariel which meant it wouldn't reach downstairs, so the tv was set up in there. Needless to say, this is also where we girls all tented to sit. It was ideal really because along with the tv you could get into the bed to keep warm. I can remember teatimes up in the room watching Harold Lloyd, or sometimes Laurel and Hardy. My mother had a large wooden tray with metal handles, and she would pile it high with bread and butter and cheese, and we would eat sandwiches in front of the telly. Bliss. My father would go mad as his bed was continually filled with crumbs. I let my kids sit in my bed and watch telly. I also complain at the crumbs, but in truth I've contributed too.

To the left of the stairs was a long corridor. This was when you went into the original house. The original stairs had been blocked off and everything downstairs from this point was left as my Granny Katherine's. We had the upstairs and a bathroom, which my father never really finished. It had a bath, but the side panel never fitted properly, and the cat was always getting stuck in the ceiling as it had a habit of crawling in through the holes made for the water pipes. He was probably following mice, but it was a regular occurrence. There were four bedrooms and so while there were five of us at home someone had to share with at least one other person at a time. We were always moving bedrooms around depending on our age or who was friends with who, but Jane never wanted to share with anyone, and if I remember rightly, she never got made to. At the time of the move to the farm I was one, Kay five, Lucy six, Rebecca ten and Jane was eleven. Very small really and what a lot had happened to them already. How mean of my father to reject them in the way that he did. Small innocent children who never asked for this, yet there they were. Rebecca had kicked up the most fuss at the move. The story goes that she had been asked what colour she wanted her new room to be, most likely in a bid to appease her by my mother. Black she had said. Dark purple was the compromise.

The original front door was still there and this lead in to where Granny Katherine lived. I can remember every detail of this house, I dream of it often and it never mutates as dreams sometimes like to do, but what I remember most of all is the smell. My son has the same recollection, and I was so deeply pleased one day when he came into my home and said this smells like Grandad's. Without fail, there was soup cooking on the hob by 11am, so if you went in the morning this is what you would smell strongly but there could be any amount of different meals cooking in that house and the smells would vary. A roast of beef, potatoes and gravy. Fresh vegetables, cakes and scones. My God, we were spoilt, and it was no different in my house next door. My mother was an exceptional cook. The smell came from the food but also the house, the walls, the floors, the grain, the bags of animal food perhaps and the muddy boots. I don't know exactly, but I can muster that up in my mind in an instant and it brings me comfort and sadness all in one go. The kitchen was a galley style and did not reflect the size of the house one bit as it was tiny and awkward to move about in.

Next to the kitchen was a dining area which housed a long wooden table and chairs. Having food at Granny Katherine's house didn't happen very often when I was a child, but if it did you were in for a treat as it usually meant some visitors were there and a party was going on. Through a tiny door into the living room not dissimilar to a Beatrix Potter illustration, another wood-burning stove was found and a window that looked out onto the lawn at the front of the house. Around the lawn a towering hedge of fir trees meant an enclosed space from the rest of the farmyard and fields around them. Granny Katherine loved her garden, and she grew vegetables and flowers. She kept it as her space and my mother never encroached upon it. The grass stretched down to the bottom of the trees and beyond them was a wall and a stream that had travelled right down from the hills. This brought the tap water to the house and cold winters and frozen pipes meant no water in the winter months if we weren't careful. Over the streams there had been a little wooden bridge. Many a game of pooh sticks had been played there and in the water, dams and paddling is a genuinely happy and strong memory for me. Remembering feeling happy is good, of course, but it also illustrates to me how that feeling happy has not been something I have experienced that much in my life. I was once asked to read a book by a psychotherapist, *The Happiness Trap* by Russ Harris I read it and thought, Listen, I am under no illusion that life is not all happy rainbows and feelings of ecstasy all the time, I don't need to read this book to find that out, but joy is something that can be felt, and I have not had enough of that emotion so far and my mind has to work at finding it.

As the years passed, the little bridge rotted away, and it was never replaced. There was nothing on the other side bar a bank of trees that you could, if you wanted to, scramble through to the road on the other side, but nobody did.

I look back on those days as good. I really do, and this tells me for sure that I can feel. I can feel and I can feel happy. I was loving life, what's not to love about a life where you can run freely in the fields, where you are safe but also fully aware of the dangers, so trusted by the adults around you to keep away from danger. This wasn't difficult though! All you had to do was stay off the roads, not go swimming in the pond alone and not stick your hand into any moving machinery. If you could manage that, which I could, you were good to go and every time you walked into the house there was food to eat, mountain water to drink and a whole bunch of sisters to spend time with if they could be bothered. I was happiest outside the house on my own, however, and perhaps the reason for this was because of all the drama and conflict going on inside. Whether it was outright arguing or unspoken resentment, it was all there.

My mother was so powerful, so protective of her girls, she never let my father in, but I wonder how much he pushed this case. My sister told me that one day my father had been telling me off and my mother had interjected as she so very often did. He said to her,

> "This one is mine, I am allowed."

When I think now about the way it feels to have another person, a man, a father, disciplining my children, I do understand, but my mother never lived long enough to learn how to let these barriers down, to trust, to let go of the power and the control. Perhaps she would have felt differently and in turn acted differently. Perhaps not.

Conversations with my sisters and their tales tell me that when they were asked to help on the farm it was very unlike the idyllic *Yorkshire Farmer* on TV that I watched recently. I watched this show and I felt quite aggrieved actually, jealous almost, and also still a little unconvinced of the actual reality of this 'reality' show. With my sisters, helping on the farm was a bit of a gamble, but the sinking feeling in your stomach as my father popped his head into the sitting room and gave the instruction, 'come here' was real. What we were going out to do could possibly involve high risk of harm or even death scenarios, or something more relaxed like helping roll up the fleeces on shearing day. My sisters told me that one day my mother told my father that enough was enough. I am going to guess it was an occasion where my father had said something along the lines of 'you are a fucking useless idiot as one of them failed to understand his muffled instructions as he walked away from them, looking in the opposite direction, and they cried in distress knowing they would inevitably fail to do what needed to be done in the correct way. From that day on he was told by my mother not to ask the girls to help on the farm and he did not. Lucky for them, not so much for me. I was his, so I had to do it. He was allowed to swear at me and call me useless and make me climb up the arm of the outstretched digger and hold the telephone pole upright while he dug it in the hole that time he was making a shed.

What I actually remember the most about my mother and father together is just that. Them sitting together. These memories probably come from the times I was a little girl, and the rest of my sisters were at school or in their rooms. I remember that they would both sit and read the paper and drink coffee together. My mother with her roll ups and my father with a slice of jam and bread. They would talk about the current affairs and books they were reading, and I would sit and listen to them. We would have lunch together, and genuinely it's a lovely memory of us three. It taught me about taking time. Not rushing through the day and always being busy. I haven't lived by that myself religiously, but they taught me that it does exist and it's something to aspire to in my opinion. People talk about how busy it is to run a farm, but the truth is there are lots of days where there isn't anything drastic or urgent to be done and it is on those days where it is important and acceptable to rest, to read your book, to speak with others, to take time to eat your lunch.

My father had not chosen the life of a farmer because of this. He loved that when it wasn't busy, he could sit and read his book, because actually the times when it was busy were pretty rubbish and the threat of your animals dying, and your crops failing was real and on his mind at all times. That's busy enough. My father hadn't really chosen to be a farmer at all and as a clever man with a lot of good ideas he could have done many more things, just like my mother. What happened instead was really I think what killed him in the end. There was so much expectation, regret, loneliness, and sadness in his soul, and it eventually caused him to take his own life.

CHAPTER SIX

As I said, my grandfather Graham, was not on the whole a kind father and was by all accounts a very poor husband to my beloved Granny Katherine. Our family, the Sutherlands will perhaps be known to you. A long line of rich farmers and landowners, a huge clan. I have in my cupboard a bag of silver cutlery with our Sutherland family crest engraved on them, but what do I do with this? Use it for eating my egg and chips this evening?

As I have been told, my grandfather's brother was a gambler, and he lost a lot of the family wealth and land, meaning that by the time I was born it was quite non-existent. My grandfather did own a farm and there was still the family home in the heart of Perthshire which I believe is now run as a B & B, but nonetheless this was the position he was in when he and my granny met and the position of the Sutherland empire. During World War Two Graham was a farmer and Katherine joined the Land Army and moved from the city of Edinburgh to the highlands of Scotland to work the land. I remember when I found out that my granny was from the city, I was gobsmacked, it just never occurred to me that she was not country born and bred as she was so connected to the land and calm in a way that city folk are not. She told me that she and her friends made sure to take a pitchfork to bed with them to ward off the farmers or the other male farm hands if they came into their bedrooms at night. What a nice reward for giving up your life and working the land for the good of Britain. My poor granny. She and my Grandad were married and lived in a remote part of the highlands on a farm called Tombreck. This is where my father was born but soon after they moved to Perthshire to the farm where I was born.

Growing up, there was my father, his older brother and his younger sister. She was a girl so of course she never got any recognition from my grandfather or probably her brothers either, but I know that she and my granny were close, and I do remember she was very protective over my granny, knowing how she suffered. On the outside of it my grandfather was a stand-up bloke. A farm owner. That always puts you top ranking. A scout leader, a good drinker, an entertainer, a father of two boys. He mixed in high society circles and went rock collecting with Prince Charles. My father told me that, in fact, he was unloving towards him. Critical. Unkind. And as for being a good husband, he would recall that my grandfather would proudly announce that he was taking his boys on a camping trip, much to their excitement, then halfway down the road they would pull over and my grandfather's latest girlfriend would jump in, and they knew then that their weekend away wasn't going to involve much father/son bonding. My grandfather got more blasé about the fact that he had girlfriends, to the point where he would simply have them in the house to stay. My beautiful strong granny had to accept it and make them their dinner. He eventually moved out or went travelling but kept just popping back in to stay when he felt like it, again bringing whoever it was that he happened to be going out with at the time with him. I can't imagine how hurtful this was for her and what it did to her self-esteem, but I will tell you this, I looked at her and I still do, as one of the strongest more admirable humans in this world. Strength of character? Most people don't have a look in when compared to her, and her kind soul was never broken by his cruelty. I am sure her soul was a bit bashed and bruised but never did she break.

Here's an interesting and brilliant twist to this tale. The first of his karmic repayments. I said that my father never really chose to be a farmer. So, as he was the second oldest, he was not in line to take over the farm, it would have been his older brother, but he didn't want to stay there and of course who can blame him, so he left and joined the Navy. He never lived back at the farm again. Grandad said to my father that if he trained as a farmer, went to agricultural college and the like, he would buy him a farm. This never happened because, well, my grandfather was mean as well as everything else. So, my father never left home, went to college, and ran the farm while my grandfather got older and then eventually moved out with his latest girlfriend and moved to Inverness. All this time he remained married to my granny, they never got divorced and, as I said, he would pop back into the farm whenever he chose because it was his and he never did get my dad his farm. His innate feeling of grandiosity meant he believed he was untouchable and that he could treat people how he liked, and there would never be any consequences. My strong mother, who never let anyone get away with anything, moved to the farm, found all of this out and did an incredible thing. She supported my granny to divorce my grandfather. She supported her to tell him that he could no longer just call in and take advantage of her kind soul and this had to stop. I honestly think that my mother must have been the only person that ever stood up to my grandfather and the funny thing is, he loved my mother possibly even more for this fact despite what happened next. The twist, I hear you ask, where is the twist? My selfish grandfather had failed to pay the correct tax support for my granny over the entirety of their married life, which was so much money that he was forced to give her the farm as settlement! The house, the farm, the stock, the contents, you name it, it was all hers. Of course, my granny in time gave the farm to my father, who also deserved it after giving up his entire life and dreams to be there. I am sure the chance to read the paper when he wanted never really cut it in the end.

My mother got cancer when I was around 7 years old, I think. I remember my older sisters getting me to make her a card and it being very unusual for her to be out of the home, but other than that it is not a distressing memory. For my mother it changed everything. In that moment she realised that she too had given up her dreams and being a farmer's wife was not what she wanted to do with her life anymore. And so, this was it, the moment when I started to feel bad, as I told my councillor, was when we moved from the farm. As much as there was all the aggravation between my sisters and my father, and indeed my father and all that he was or wasn't to me, the farm was a sanctuary to me. The land, the safety, the air, the water, the earth. My roots firmly set in this space so abruptly ripped out.

My mother, even though she had not been diagnosed as terminally ill at this time, quite rightly, wanted to spend the rest of her life living. She saw living as seeing people, going to the theatre, visiting museums and all of these sorts of things. She also believed that moving away from the farm would be good for us girls.

CHAPTER SEVEN

My sisters are significant people to me, I can't write a book about my life and leave them out. Jane is my oldest sister and also my mother substitute. At the farm, my memories of her are few. I remember when she cut my hair into a cute little bob, I liked that, and I remember at Christmas she wouldn't get out of bed in the morning to open presents which I couldn't understand, and I remember I used to ask to sleep in her bed, as her room was really tidy, and I liked that. She had a double bed, I think, or it seemed big to me, and I never liked to sleep alone. She said I could if I didn't 'niggle' which meant move around. I couldn't not niggle, so she didn't very often say yes, but I liked her a lot, she was very safe and reliable. She moved out and went to university when I was still very young but visiting her in the big city was a lot of fun. My mum dropped me off there once on our way back from a holiday and I stayed in her student flat with her and her friends for a few days. She took me shopping and I bought some hair setting lotion for my Cindy doll, then we watched Live Aid on the telly. I thought they were all so cool and their hair was cool, and they had cool clothes. This is how our relationship continued, I'd see her here and there at one student flat and the next. It was her that told me about periods and about having to wear deodorant. My mother didn't talk about that sort of thing, and she wouldn't have ever bought us toiletries or Tampax! Goodness knows how I managed to scramble my way through life and get these items. I do know actually. I stole them from the shops or my friends' houses. I made sanitary towels with toilet roll and Sellotape and very often sat with wet uncomfortable clothes, too afraid and embarrassed to ask anyone for help. Who would I ask? I still don't know the answer to that if truth be known. My mother was a lovely mother. I don't know what that was about and why she did that to me, but I had Jane.

Rebecca is next and I have fewer memories of her as a child. She had loads of rabbits and gerbils at the farm, I remember that, and she was good at art. This pleased my mother greatly and she was supported in any way possible to pursue this at university, which she did in London and lived there until she had two children and moved to Spain with them and her partner. She and my dad had a huge fight, I don't know what happened, but it wasn't long before she left for London, and they never spoke again. I always thought it was strange when I saw her sobbing almost at my father's funeral. She was kind to me; I remember that much, and I remember we would go for little picnics in the woods. One time we sat in the fields, and we looked for four-leaf clovers. I found one and so did she. That's how I remember it. I wished for a pet lamb, and she said that wasn't a good thing to wish for because it meant the lamb didn't have a mummy. She said she wished to leave the farm and I thought, why do you want to leave me? I know that my sisters had a hard time living there and with my father. I was sorry about that. I never in my life thought of them as half-sisters, they were my sisters. Yet my father, who I was attached to, was unkind to them. It never made me feel good and I felt the energy was attached to me. I built up the courage once, brought from pure anger, to say something to him. It was years after we had all left and I was an adult. He was making some sort of derogatory remark about one of them. I turned to him as we sat together in the van up on the hill, after chasing around for some sheep. The snow was thick on the ground and my hands were frozen as I tried to warm them in my pockets. Already my senses were heightened by the extreme cold, and I said to him,

"They are my sisters, you know."

I was loud and I was abrupt in my tone. I looked straight at him, and he looked straight back at me, which was something my father rarely did, and he looked shocked. He was shocked, and while I didn't say many words, I got my message across, and I do believe he heard me. I said to him that they were part of me, part of my family. By hurting them he hurt me. By being rude about them, he was rude to me. My father never gave much thought about how rude he was to me of course. I was his though, wasn't I?

What I would say about my sister, Lucy, now is that she is one of the toughest yet calmest people ever to walk this earth. Wow is she fearsome. Hmm, I'm sensing a theme here with these women in my family. Spending time with Lucy is always fun and relaxed, she is a really good laugh despite her rather practical looking appearance. Lucy makes her own clothes, and what she wears is smart, but with an injection of uniqueness in an interesting fabric. She has long ginger hair which she wears in a long plait, and she wouldn't be interested in wearing any make up or having a painted nail. When she was younger though she wore the most make up of us all, punk style with bright red hair and a good helping of black eyeliner. At the farm we didn't really spend much time together. She found me irritating, I think, and in truth she was quite cruel to me, winding me up and making me cry with her sharp words. Harsh might be the right word for Lucy at times. She does not suffer fools, she really does not, and while that may lead you to think that she is unempathetic, the contrary applies, and she is extremely understanding and caring. I think the issue comes if she has listened to you, offered advice with exact instructions and then you choose not to follow it. In this case you are entirely responsible for the outcome, so her cup of empathy is empty, and you are on your own. I appreciate that I know where I am with Lucy and our relationship developed long after we had both left home, as at times she has supported me incredibly with wise words, often ones that I didn't like to hear but needed to, and in practical ways that I will be forever grateful for. I am sad to say that again we don't speak like we used to. I miss her and often think that perhaps her cup of empathy for me is empty, and I could understand that. She did live with us until she moved to Edinburgh to retake her A-levels. I remember it was quite a family scandal that she didn't pass them all. She was a bit of a rebel with her make up and her boyfriends. You know the normal stuff that a large proportion of teenagers partake in, but honestly this was considered delinquent in my family and then she didn't pass all her A-levels – the shame! Knowing what I know now about Lucy, I bet that she took this negativity and bottled it up into a big 'fuck you' and carried on to lead an extremely successful life. Success is objective, but to me and her, the life she has cocreated for herself is successful. She does what she chooses with whom she chooses. Successful.

Rebecca and her partner had two children, My beautiful niece and nephew who I love dearly. I always have a special space in my heart for my neice. Just before a visit to London to see her as a newborn baby I had lost a baby of my own. I didn't tell anyone apart from Lucy and didn't tell Rebecca as that would be upsetting for her and ruin her own happy news. This baby, that I could hold and cuddle and feel in my arms, well, it nearly broke my heart in two to leave her at the end of that visit. Rebecca has had a pretty tough run of luck herself. She is just recovering from a second dose of breast cancer and processing a whole lot of other things, I am sure. We have been closer due to the children and being the only mothers among the sisters, not technically but yes, the only mothers taking care of their children. I wish she would spend less time in the past, but I suppose we are all on our own healing pathway and she is working through that part. Healing, finding peace, whatever you want to call it, it happens at your own pace, that's a fact, even if the people around you want it to be different.

Sweet little Kay, that's what my mother would call her. And she was sweet, very cute, a round face, blue eyes, blond hair and quiet as a mouse. She sat and she got on with some intricate crafting and she did the dishes and she made everyone cups of coffee and she never made a fuss. This girl was throughout my life my absolute rock, I do not know how I would have fared without her. When she moved away, I felt like a part of my lifeforce had been cut off, I cannot fully express how much I miss her to this day and what an impact she had in my life, but she left me.

Kay had a son. She was not able to look after him and that is the short version of the tale. I asked social services if I could care for him, but they ignored me. They judged me as unfit as well as Kay with her mental illness and her husband with whatever horrors he was carrying with him. How ironic that in a couple of years from then I would be one of them. A social worker. When they took him away, I was inconsolable.

Poor Kay, just poor poor Kay, she got just about the shittiest end of a stick you could even imagine, if you judge life by the amount of shit there is on your stick. Imagine if that was really how it was dealt out. Life. Someone, let's say the person in charge, God perhaps, they choose a stick for each person and lace it with varying amounts of shit that they perhaps think you deserve or don't, or need to learn from, and then hand them out to you and that's it, the stick has been dealt and you have to deal with it. The shit.

When I was a little girl, my mother compared me to the other girls. They were the girls, and I was Silvia. They were all clever, I was not. They were all well behaved, I was naughty. They all went to bed and read books, I did not. They all managed to speak to family members or the lady in the shop. I did not. My words did not come out.

    "I was sad when I saw I had given birth to another girl", she said one day to her friend, "But I needn't have worried, Silvia is as wild as a boy."

I mean, that sentence in itself could take a whole chapter to digest and unpick, but this was the general message I was receiving. The pet-name given to me by my mother was Tarzan. I flew about, I didn't sit still long enough to learn how to knit as well as my sisters or to sew as neatly. I rushed through and enjoyed kicking a ball about in the farmyard, driving about on the side of the tractor with my father or making a damn in the stream much more. I never wanted to go to bed, and I would get up and shout at the top of the stars for someone to come and see me. I cried myself to sleep, eventually calming down, and watching the light outside my room with the door slightly ajar through tear-filled eyes. I didn't want to be there alone going to sleep in the dark, my eyes were open. Of course, I know now what was going on with that little girl. Kay helped me though it all. In the morning I would be tired after spending the night crying and playing and getting up and down the stairs, and I found school boring and difficult, so I never wanted to go. Kay would help me. She would sit with me and reassure me. She would get my clothes and even dress me some days. I am not even sure if my mother was aware that all of this was happening, these relationships between us, these negotiations between us. I don't even remember her getting me out of bed at all, it was always Kay. My mother was usually in the kitchen having some sort of argument with my older sisters or dishing out the bowls of porridge and plates of toast. Kay knew that my mother would hit the roof if I didn't get out of bed and go to school, which she would, so she saved me, and the pair of us arrived at the table and ate our food before being driven to the next little village, where we caught the school bus. There was a school nearer in the village where we lived but my mother fell out with the teacher there, so we weren't to go. At school I would regularly forget my books, my pencil, my knickers even on occasion. We would have to get changed for gym and I'd realise, and Kay would help me, covering me while I put on my shorts. It never occurred to me to ask anyone else for help, not even my mother, because I never had to. That is until Kay left and went to high school, and I really started to get into trouble. I didn't really care though and, even then, I was aware that this was not quite right. I just could not muster up the emotion to care, and it continued, my apathy towards school and the consequences for my action in general, but there was a lot more going on by then which didn't help. It just made me want to get up for school even less. One year my school report came through and my parents talked openly about it in front of me in the van on the way home from the school.

"Average" my mother said incredulously "Average for everything! How can she be average for absolutely everything?"

Being average was basically being an absolute loser in my mother's opinion. Give up now Silvia, you are absolutely shit, is what I heard.

CHAPTER EIGHT

On the weeks building up to our move to Newcastle my mother talked to me about what it would be like, and I was quite excited. She used to read me the *Milly Molly Mandy* books and she told me that when we moved to the town this is what it would be like. *Milly Molly Mandy* was first published in 1925 and was about a little girl who in the main ran errands for her mother or her granny for little somethings from the shops along the street, such as a loaf of bread or a piece of fabric, and she walked there freely knowing all the neighbours and the shop keepers, and she went on little adventures around the streets and it was as nice an image as I could imagine for a place to live apart from where I lived at the time, which I loved. I was pretty sold on this idea and prepared to give it a go.

I hadn't seen the house before we moved there but she told me about it, and it was a lot like the terraced houses in the *Milly Molly Mandy* books. That part was kind of true, sort of, well quite vaguely, yes, not really like *Milly Molly Mandy* apart from that it was a house in a street. We didn't live there straight away. Because the house sale was dragging a bit as they often do, my mother was worried that we were going to miss the start of the school term, so we stayed in a holiday house for a couple of weeks before we actually moved to our new *Milly Molly Mandy* house.

This was step one in my disdain for this house move. The holiday house was a long way from where we lived, so we had to get up super early to get the metro to school. This was torture for me right away. The next awful step into the reality of this situation: The new school. My mother hadn't followed the instructions given about school uniform. It said blue or white shirt. She had been over the moon to find in the charity shop a blue and white checked shirt and put me in that. She made my school skirt so it stuck out at a strange angle, and she hadn't got me any white socks, so on my first day of school I turned up in my red sandals, green socks, a checky shirt and the school jumper at least. I had a weird Scottish accent, and I was in for my first big lesson in life. Nobody at primary school wants to be friends with the weirdo dressed like a refugee who sounds like Supergran. This had never happened to me before. Yes, I always hated school for all of the reasons I have told you so far, but it was never because my friends were horrible to me or because I had nobody to play with! I probably did look like a tattie-bogle every day who didn't even remember to put her knickers on, but I was fully accepted. Not any more sweetheart. That ship had sailed, and I was an outcast.

One girl finally spoke to me. Tiana, whose parents were from Pakistan. Sadly, but truthfully, because of her colour and race she was an outcast along with me. This was our connection, both of us were different, neither of us fitted into the norm of the typically middle-class white family that sent their children to this school. My mother was overjoyed firstly that I had made a friend, secondly that I had not made a friend with all the 'normal' children and thirdly that my friend was in fact so unusual. So far, I hadn't met anyone who was a different religion or a different culture, whose parents spoke a different language, so my mother was telling everyone she could. I could hear her on the phone telling this story, making up the narrative that everything was working out so well in this new town and with this new life, but for me it was not. I had no objection to being friends with Tiana, she was nice, and her family were really lovely and kind. She was part of this multi-cultural club that used to go on trips to the seaside or the illuminations and she invited me along and I was extremely pleased about being included, but I wasn't accepted there either. I was, to them, a white middle-class girl who knew nothing of their cultural struggles in this Northern city, which was true, I did not. I was not really part of the gang, so I still fitted nowhere it felt to me. I wanted more than anything to be part of the normal kid's gang. I wanted to have brushed hair in the latest hairstyle, which was at the time a side ponytail and if you were really on trend, you had a banana clip. I longed for a banana clip. I wanted to have the same school uniform as everyone else that had been bought from the local shop on the high street where everyone else bought theirs. I wanted a clear plastic school bag that you could get for 3.99 in the market and was the same as all the other girls in my class. I wanted to look nice, to scrub my stupid Scottish freckles off my face and pull out my stupid ginger hair that everyone teased me for. I wanted to have 50p in my pocket and to join my friends when they went to the paper shop for sweets but since we had moved to an actual town and it was not 1925 my mother was suddenly terrified to let me run freely anywhere and I so desperately wanted to 'call on a friend' and hang out, perhaps listening to pop music wearing some cool outfit that was… yes, Mother, the same as everyone else's. I did not want to be different; I did not want to stand out. I wanted to be accepted. The worst days of my primary school days were without a doubt, 'wear what you want days.' Wear your own clothes to school, what fun! Now we may have lived in a nice house in a nice part of town, but money was not available to us. My mother had left her husband without a job. I actually don't know the ins and outs of it – the downfall of half your family being dead before you find this sort of thing out – but from what I can gather, my sisters' grandfather bought the house that we moved into in Newcastle. He also gave my mother money for my sisters' future which she had in a savings account. When my mother tried to claim benefits for us to live on as she had no job, and no husband, she told them about these savings for their future and they wouldn't give her anything. I remember hearing snippets of these conversations as a child, and I listened out for them because, in one fell swoop, everything I knew to be certain in my life changed so I was on high alert for anything that would help me make sense of it all.

We didn't have any money, this was what became apparent, so the £3.99 bag from the market was not happening. Even if my mother had wanted to, the possibility of getting anything slightly acceptable to wear on 'come as you fucking please day' at school, was non-existent. My poor little inner child still feels sad about this next tale.

In the holidays, I had been bought a pair of pyjamas during a trip to visit an older relative on my mother's side. They were from a shop in China Town, pale pink cotton pyjamas. In 1986 pastels were in fashion so my little brain had what it conceived as a brilliant idea. I could wear these pyjama bottoms to school and pretend they were trousers. I have wiped from my mind what I dragged from the depths of my wardrobe to wear as my top, but off I went in these garments. My mother saw me and allowed me to walk out the door that day and go to school. I wore my red shoes, because in those days you had one pair of shoes that you wore until they were outgrown and then you got another pair, not lots of pairs of shoes that you could wear for different outfits or activities. I went to school feeling like I had succeeded in looking ok for this enforced event. First, I saw the sniggering. Then I saw the pointing. I walked to my desk, but my heart was beating, and my feet didn't feel like they were mine anymore because my soul was dissociating itself as fast as it could from this increasingly distressing situation. My soul knew that something bad was afoot, even though it wasn't quite sure what exact horror was about to unfold. I could feel the eyes of everyone in my class staring at me, and I just looked down. To my right, I caught the eye of a girl who looked at me and I saw genuine sympathy in her expression. She came over to me and knelt down by my side, I remember it clear as day.

"You can see your knickers," she whispered.

Oh my God, I nearly died on the spot, but it was worse, because I thought she meant that my knickers were somehow popping out the back of my trousers, so I frantically struggled to feel and push them back in.

"No" she said, "through your pants, you can see your knickers!"

I looked down and she was right. These paper-thin cotton pyjamas that were not trousers, were showing my entire underwear though them. This gets worse. On the front of these knickers was a picture of a little girl on a swing under a tree. If you were born in the seventies, you will know the ones I am referring to and there they were, in full view of my class. I had nowhere to go and nothing that I could do about it. You know those dreams where you find yourself naked at school or at work? This was happening in full technicolour reality, and I couldn't make it stop by opening my eyes. Looking back, thank God this was a day that I remembered to wear underwear at all, but why did nobody save me? Not one teacher saved me when they could have. My mother did not save me. Why? Nobody is going to save you. Memo from the universe, I get it now.

Days that I messed up, got it wrong, embarrassed myself beyond recognition, continued throughout primary school. 'Traumatic days I have had at school', might be the title for my next book, but the short version is that a solid 4 years of this seriously damaged my confidence. My self-worth, my self-esteem, was already fragile, hanging on by an unfashionable thread, and then I went to high school, YOU ARE UGLY, NOBODY LIKES YOU, YOU ARE AN EMBARASSMENT AND STUPID firmly locked in the core belief section of my mind.

Despite my bashed soul I am an optimist, I am, and I knew that I had some hope of turning this around if I managed to do a few things right on my first day at high school. My main aim was to become part of a group and not an outcast. In order to do that I had to drop Tiana and I carried the guilt for that for a very long time, but I was desperate, and I was only 13 years of age. I can forgive myself now. I knew that I needed to somehow get the right outfit to wear and by an ingenious feat of stealth and guts I got my father to hand over £50 to me for new school clothes. £50!!! I can still hardly believe it, but this was such a golden opportunity I feel the gratitude still. I bought myself some black tights, a short mini skirt; navy blue, so it was classed as uniform, an actual shirt from the actual school shirt shop, a baggy navy-blue v neck jumper which if I was confident enough, I could pull off the shoulder, looking even more trendy than I could allow my little mind to believe, and black lace up boots. I even had enough to buy a super cool school bag, the ones from the Indian shops that were made of fabric and had embroidery and little mirrors sewn into the front of them, and, to top off the look, a mascara, and a black eye liner. I had some hope on the first day of school and, while I hadn't fully banked on the wrath of the 'Sharons' as they were known, I was making a better start than last time.

The 'Sharons,' their male counterpart being the 'Trevors', were a group of girls that wore inches of orange foundation and even the teachers were afraid to tell them not to. They had a perm, bleached hair if they were really high up in the ranks and trainers the height of a seventies platform, and they gave zero fucks about the rule that said no trainers were allowed. Even these frightsome girls were small fry when compared with the relentless grief I had received in primary, plus I was growing hard and tough. Was that what it was? Toughness?

I knew that I was never going to fit in as high up as a Sharon, but a hippy, grungy vibe was a good shot, and this was an actual group that people belonged to, so that was decided. My older sisters were in this group and, while they also got spat at by the Sharons, they had survived.

This is when and how I met my best friend in the world, Emma. Emma had blond curly hair, she wore black boots, black tights, had a cool denim jacket and liked Guns and Roses. She had come from a different primary school where she had a firm set of friends who all had similar looks and an interest in Guns and Roses. Becoming friends with Emma gave me an entry into this group. A mix of girls who all seemed out of my league. They had boys' attention, something that had passed me by so far and a few of them even had boyfriends, I mean, their level of cool was off the scale to me. No boy would ever look in my direction and if they did it was only to laugh. Most of this group lived in big houses and had lots of pocket money and nice clothes, apart from me and Emma, and I think this is how we began to bond initially. They went on shopping trips to town and bought things such as make up and clothes. We tagged along with only enough cash for a bag of chips if we were lucky and I got caught shoplifting VO5 Hot Oils and spent the afternoon in a police cell with a caution on my record to show for it. It was a clear line between us, despite the many nights we spent together, first at each other's houses for sleepovers then to house parties then to underage nights out to the pub and nightclubs.

I started high school when I was thirteen with no friends and no plan or care for the future other than to be accepted and have friends! At age 16, I was pregnant and living away from my family, with no money, and the few friends I had managed to secure, including Emma, went on to live their lives and I was left behind.

CHAPTER NINE

So, I had never had any interest from boys before I started high school, although I had wished and wondered. A couple of boys in my class that all the girls fancied, I saw them too, but I knew, or I *believed*, they would never have any interest in me, and so far, I had been proved right.

"You're right, Brigid, the bairn is fair putting on the beef" my granny had said during a visit to our house one day.

Confirmation. I was fat, even my family were talking about it. In the eighties being fat meant being unattractive, it was to be avoided at all costs and, as well as being ginger, having a strange Scottish accent, being thick and unpopular, I was now also fat. What, as a hypnotherapist, I know now, is that this one single event, a single sentence, can plant an idea and a belief in a person's mind that sticks. This remark from my granny, and all the things so far combined, cemented the belief in my mind. Here's the thing, I was a perfectly healthy weight, and it's so common for me in my work to support women to unpick and undo the lifelong damage caused by these messages we were given. Because this message was for everyone, the definitions of beauty that we must obtain in order to be happy and accepted. We don't decide what these are, these are decided for us, and we must get into line (starve ourselves) if we are to be loved.

I looked at the boys and fantasised about a possible kiss or words of affection from one of them, but they never looked back. By a stroke of luck, I had managed to infiltrate a group of friends who were, on the whole, confident self-assured girls, and this meant opportunities to be in the company of boys. This to me was both exciting and terrifying.

"Don't you find yourself in a room alone with a boy!" my mother said to me, or rather shouted at me one day, because all he would want to do is have sex with me. Obviously, I had no power over this. The boy had all the power and I had to hope that this just never happened, or this terrible act would simply occur. I know what she was trying to do. She was trying to protect me from what had undoubtedly happened to her, but her words were full of blame. You are responsible first of all for this. If you do fail at this crucial stage, then anything that happens next is completely your fault and completely out of your control. Men have all the control, you have none. This is what I heard; this is what I believed.

At school there were rules around boys. You couldn't fancy the same boy as one of your friends. You could kiss a boy without this meaning you were in a relationship, but this one often got confused by both sides. Kissing too many boys made you a slag. Having sex with a boy made you either a hero or a slag depending on who was making the judgment. You could have sex with your boyfriend, but it might be that you have misread the boyfriend/girlfriend status and were therefore at high risk of being a slag.

The first time I kissed a boy was at a party that I had lied about going to, as became usual practice, because my mother would have simply said no and, look, I wasn't going to give up the chance of going to a party if I actually got invited to one! I fancied this boy, and this message was conveyed to him, this is how it worked. Looking back, I actually didn't! I didn't find this boy attractive at all, but remember the rule where you couldn't fancy the same boy as one of your friends? Well, all the boys I fancied had been claimed and he was the only one left. How unkind to this poor boy. We were shoved into a room together which was what happened at this type of party, as I discovered, and there I was. I had found myself in a room alone with a boy. Shit. How had this happened? How could I be so stupid, how could I have allowed this to spiral so disastrously? I had had to choose someone to fancy, I went with him, and don't you know it, he actually had a vague interest in kissing me. Should I be happy? Isn't this what I had wanted for a long time, someone to fancy me? We did kiss and by pure damn luck he did not attempt to have sex with me.

A few days later I was told, in the brutal manner I became accustomed to, that he didn't actually fancy me, he fancied my friend. She kissed him at the next party. Where was the rule about that?

The thing about going to parties is that there was always drink and drugs and me and alcohol – or drugs – have never been a good mix. As a teenager they gave me a boost of confidence which I hadn't managed to gather so far, and when I say confidence, what I really mean is my impulsive nature was heightened, and by that, I mean that I regularly did reckless and embarrassing things. I didn't follow the boy rules which meant I was quite often at the mercy of being a slag, a bad friend, an outcast, a mess, a liability.

Subsequently, I wasn't always included, and this hurt, and I was constantly at risk of losing all that I had managed to find. I just didn't understand the rules, I always did the wrong thing, and it was because I was disempowered. It never occurred to me that I was in control of any situation which left me feeling very out of control and scared. Scared people can act recklessly.

The first time I had sex with a boy I was at a friend's house, it is a classic example of this recklessness, and I was only 14 years old. Again, there was this strange conversation that went on between your friends that brought messages from the boys to the girls or vice versa. I suppose this replaced a text message or a snapchat that would be used by teenagers today, but the reason remained the same. None of us were mature enough or had the capabilities of having these conversations face to face. The friends, the messages, the system we had instilled, that was in control of these situations. The boy I had sex with was someone who we didn't know, just an older boy who was there. He liked me apparently and actually he was a good-looking boy and so I was quite taken a back that he had an interest in me. So, I found myself in a room alone with a boy again, and if I understood this correctly then once again, I had failed to stop this from happening and once again I was in the power of this boy. It so happened that this boy did want to have sex with me so that is what happened. This bothered me and still does, for countless reasons, but the main one is this. I had no emotion about this event. I simply felt nothing in my mind, in my soul, in my heart, about what was happening. It felt neither pleasurable nor awful in the physical sense and then it was over, and we left the room. My friends huddled around me, I remember, asking me what had happened and as I told them they were all giddy and talkative and emotional about it. How strange I thought. What is the big deal here? Despite his good looks this boy was a bit of a shit. We had sex a couple more times and I naively thought we were in a relationship because of this, but we were not. Got it wrong again. He was outwardly unkind to me. He would appear in the group wherever it might be that we were hanging out that weekend and sometimes he spoke, and sometimes he didn't. I didn't have the capacity to talk to him about this and it seemed that neither did he as eventually he told Emma to tell me to leave him alone as if I was some crazed stalker. Forgive me for thinking I meant even a little bit to you at the age of fourteen. My next encounter, and I say encounter because again this was never a nice kind of relationship, was with a boy much older than me who didn't even go to school. He would use me for sex when he wanted it and when he didn't or he was having sex with another girl, he ignored me. That's the bare facts of the situation, but my young romantic self was obviously obsessed with him and made all sorts of excuses for his behaviour towards me. I would ring him from the phone box, and he would entertain me most of the time. I wonder as I write this if this pattern has continued. Hanging on to every small positive moment and ignoring the rest. Wishful thinking, a need to be loved, these are factors, I am sure. He isn't unkind to me all of the time, I'd say to myself. There was that time last week when he smiled at me, I think that must mean he really likes me deep down. I didn't trust my intuition very much until recently, but when a person offers you scraps of their affection, they don't really like you, and your intuition, that sensation right in your solar plexus will tell you that. You may not listen but that is the message.

Emma stuck by me, and she never called me silly although she probably thought it, I am sure. She has a way with words, a way of guiding you without being judgmental but also of saying what needs to be said. My reckless soul would listen sometimes and when I didn't, she cared for me anyway. Each day I would meet Emma at the bus stop and the aim was that we would walk to school together. I never wanted to go to school, and I really didn't care about what happened to me if I didn't go. I would persuade Emma to skip school with me even when she decided she wanted to go. When she got caught, she cared, and she didn't want to upset her mother anymore. I knew I was upsetting my mother, but I was prepared to live through the speeches and the shouting if it meant I didn't have to go.

All I ultimately cared about was getting to Friday night where we could go out. Go to the park, go to a house party, sit in someone's room and get stoned. Some really shit and boring things to do but I was in need of a hit, something that made me feel, feel something at all, and for then that was it.

CHAPTER TEN

I understand a little bit now about what this needing a hit was, as painful as that hit may have been. I wanted a hit of fun and excitement which I was getting from the drink and the drugs and the kissing of the boys, even if they didn't actually fancy me or I them, but I also wanted to escape my life at home. At age 14, there were only two of my sisters left living at home. They had friends, went to the pub, went to college, I don't know. They had boyfriends, and quite rightly were engaged with their own lives, and while they helped me slightly with makeup and clothes, they didn't have the time or the patience for me.

By the time I was fifteen they had both left home, so it was just me and my mother. My mother became unwell. I knew it was cancer, but I had no idea what this meant and none of the adults around me took the time to explain. I assumed that even though she was ill, she was going to hospital, and she would recover at some point, but in the meantime, she was pretty incapacitated as a mother. She would go into hospital for her treatment then come home and be unwell for days. Being sick, sleeping, looking weird, losing her hair. My mother was always the sort of mother that had food in the cupboards and tea on the table for us, but those days of a house filled with the inviting smells of delicious meals were long gone. We had been spoilt with our fresh produce readily available on the farm and now, with very little money to live on, the notion of a roast pheasant and seasonal vegetables followed by a bowl of homemade ice cream or a plum pie was down the smelly drain outside in the smoggy street we now lived in. Suddenly I came home and there was no food and no tea cooking. This was disconcerting and I felt very alone. I was angry at my mother, not because she didn't cook my tea but because it had all changed and who else could I be angry with. She wouldn't tell anyone, she was ashamed. I began to do the shopping, to sort out the bills to clean the house, to take care of it all. She shared with me, and I feel so sorry because she must have felt very alone too. I was a shitty teenager, and I was angry at her and left her at every opportunity. One day she asked me to make her mushrooms on toast. I went down and made a beautiful mushroom sauce and took it proudly up to her on her toast. Oh, she said, I meant just fried mushrooms on toast, I can't eat the creamy sauce, I'm so sorry. I knew she was sorry; I knew it was her treatment and her stomach was sensitive. I stomped down the stairs with the plate and smashed it off the kitchen wall.

In the months that my mother was unwell people would come to visit and my uncle arranged a couple of holidays for her. When they would visit, she would perk up and be all jolly. This made me even more angry with her. Oh, so you can laugh and joke with them and enjoy a glass of wine, but you can't even get out of bed for me? They would move things around in my kitchen and cook food that we didn't enjoy. They would talk to me like a child and go quiet when I walked into the room, as if what they were talking about was too shocking for my young sensitive ears to hear. Listen here, I thought, I have spent the last week listening to her throw her guts up, running around making her any amount of mushroom on toast variations, sitting for 2 hours on the phone to British gas trying to sort out this latest bill that we can't pay, and that's not to mention that I've not been to school, I've been having sex with a boy way older than me who is in truth abusing me, spent a couple of days off my head on acid wandering around the dene with people I didn't know, smoking rollies out my bedroom window listening to Pink Floyd and thinking of ways to kill myself. Whatever you have to say, I can cope. What they were in fact probably talking about was the news that my mother was not going to live. She was not going to recover. My sister told me a few years later that they all knew. I was furious. Why did they choose to keep this from me? Regret is a damaging emotion. Years and years I carried profound regret and guilt about the way I treated my mother in those last few months. That I left her alone, that I was angry at her for being ill. What I would have given to go back and stay at home, safe, with her eating chocolate and watching Poirot on the TV. What I wouldn't give now to pop round my mother's for a cup of coffee and a natter about the kids, or my life, or my job, or almost anything. What I wouldn't give to just say hello to her.

Christmas came and my mother was in hospital, so I rashly decided to go stay with my father. I hadn't spent Christmas with my father since we had left the farm and I instantly regretted my decision, but there you go. Not even my lovely Granny Katherine was there, she had gone to Edinburgh to spend Christmas with her sister. This crushed my heart; she knew I was coming but still went away anyway. Rejection. This is how it felt at the time. Inevitably I was given the job of cooking the dinner, but I persuaded him to buy some decorations which we put up and it felt a little better. We did have a nice day, we did, and it's a good memory that I have banked in my heart about my father. When I returned, my sisters who had come home for a week or so, and I went to see my mum in the hospital for 'Christmas' and we opened a few presents. I did not enjoy this. I was reminded of how depressing it had been when I eventually became a social worker and at Christmas, we would arrange visits for children and their parents in some grotty room in a rundown family centre with no home comforts. Trying to make out that this was a fun experience for the kids, bring a small amount of joy into a situation that was soul destroying for everyone.

CHAPTER ELEVEN

My sister Kay took acid one night that triggered schizophrenia and sent her down a rabbit hole that she never returned from. Even so, she moved into a flat in the west end of Newcastle while she was at college getting her qualifications for uni. That was what she had to do, that was the route that everyone took, so this remained the plan. I started having to look out for her as well as my mother. She was so unwell, but my mother was in denial. She thought that if we sought care she would be locked away and she would never get out like the film, *One Flew Over the Cuckoo's Nest*. My mother never lived to see what happened, but *One Flew Over the Cuckoo's Nest* was a picnic compared to the reality of what this poor soul has gone through since. Sweet little Kay didn't deserve this. On the day we were going to the hospital for 'Christmas' I was set with the task of persuading Kay to take a bath. When you're living in a psychotic state, your personal hygiene is not always a priority, and I don't think she had washed for weeks. My mother would have been upset to see her like this, I knew this much, so I tried to wash her. She didn't want me to, and I shouted at her in desperation,

"Get in the bath, you can't go out like this! You smell, people are looking at you!" I screamed, and eventually she gave in.

I would despair at the state of Kay for myself sometimes. I was trying my best to fit in, to look like everyone else, and here she was walking down the street in a mishmash of clothes, no bra, unwashed, talking nonsense at the top of her voice. Basically, a person with a severe mental illness, but I didn't know that and most people in society don't know that either, so they look, and they point, and they laugh. Once you do know, by the way, it is very hard not to spot a person with this level of illness. I see them and they see me seeing them, so they always talk. In a way I am grateful for my understanding and my experience because it allows me to ignore the 'unusual' behaviour that you see first and listen to the person beneath.

So, on this stressful day, I presented her to the rest of the family as we met at the hospital. She still looked pretty weird, and I hadn't fully managed to get her into clean clothes or brush her hair very well so it wasn't exactly a surprise reveal like you see on those makeover shows, but she was there, and my mother would have been pleased, nonetheless.

New Year passed, and school started again. My mother hadn't been able to come home and for a change Jane had come to stay to look after me. Ah, the irony. Knowing what I know now, this must have been because they knew my mother wasn't coming out. I hadn't been to visit her for a few days, the hospital smelt strange and was boring to be honest. I never really visited at the other times so why should I now? I was sitting on the Sunday evening before the start of school, which I was going to have to go to since my sister was there, and I suddenly realised I hadn't seen my mother for what seemed like a really long time.

"Can we go and visit mum?" I asked.

"Yes," she said, and we got up immediately and went.

She knew, and I often wonder, did my mother wait for me? Did she send me a message somehow telling me to come? If I hadn't gone that day, I wouldn't be able to remember the last time I had seen her.

We walked into her room. She had moved, she was in a room on her own and as I walked up to her, I was shocked. She looked dead. That's what I thought, her face drawn and wrinkled like a skeleton. She had a drink of water next to her and in it this plastic fish that squeezed water out its mouth if you filled it up. A toy? I was confused. My sister told me my mother had been using it to drink water from as she couldn't lift the glass. She knew this as she had been visiting each day when I had not. I pulled it out and asked her if she wanted a drink. She barely spoke, she mumbled at me and closed her eyes.

"Wake up!" I said. "WAKE UP!"

I needed her to wake up, but she kept closing her eyes. I was so angry, it filled me up like a furnace inside my body, so forceful I imagine I could have blown flames from my mouth, so I squeezed the water in her face, right at her. Have that, I thought, but she hardly stirred. Right, I thought, if you can't even wake up when I've come to visit, I'm leaving, and I walked out. My sister came after me. I felt in my pocket for my sandpaper. I had developed this habit of grinding sandpaper between my teeth, which nobody noticed, but was a reflection of the extreme stress I was under.

"Are you okay?" she said, and she wasn't angry at me.

"Yes," I said, and I felt tears trying to pop out of my

face.

I pushed them right back in. I WILL NOT CRY. There was no point. I cried to alert my mother that I needed help. She was not going to save me today, so there was no point.

The next day I went to school, I remember feeling very subdued that morning, I hadn't the energy to make up a scheme to get out of it and I wasn't up for sitting in the cold somewhere for a day, so I went and stayed there until the end of the day, then I walked slowly home. I had a sense of not wanting to go home, I remember it quite clearly in my body, the feeling of slowness, of reluctance to take those steps along my street and up to the front door. I knew. Jane opened the door just as I put my key in the lock.

"Mum's died," she blurted out at me.

"You're joking," I said, which was a fairly ridiculous response as this was simply not the kind of thing my sister would joke about, and it was no joke. My mother had died. I stormed past her. My granny was in the sitting room, I could hear her voice, but I didn't want to see her. I went up the stairs and to my room. I can recall every detail of this moment; I walked over to my chest of drawers and rolled a cigarette. I lit it up and smoked it right there in my room when usually I'd hang out of the window at least. I heard voices downstairs, my granny was leaving, so I went down and sat on the stairs as she was getting her coat on. My granny looked at me and said,

"Oh, look at you, sitting all sloppy right there," sounding disgusted.

Excuse me? My granny had a sharp tongue at times, and she had just lost her daughter, but did she think this was the best time for it? Well, that was what she said, and then she left.

By this time Kay had moved to Bradford, despite how ill she was they had shoved her away to university in Bradford, because this was more important than anything. I'm sure the psychosis was just going to pass as she sat alone in a strange city with new people and about to embark upon a 3-year degree in fine art. Yes, that would all work out well. We decided that we couldn't ring Kay with the news so our neighbour agreed to drive Jane to Bradford to get her. I was left in the care of my sisters boyfriend, so I was safe. He was not going to invade my space and start trying to ask me how I was feeling, and this was ideal as far as I was concerned. As soon as they all left, I went upstairs, and I cried and cried and then I rang Emma, and I told her what had happened. She got on the bus and came to get me. In the night I heard Kay being brought back home. I prayed to just sleep. I didn't want to open my eyes the next day to this.

The days and weeks that followed my mother's death were strange, as you might expect. All my sisters were at home again and preparations for the funeral were happening. I stayed in with my family for a while, but I couldn't really stand all the noise and the people, so it wasn't long before I escaped out again. My friends didn't know what to say and I was glad because I didn't know what to say had they spoken to me about it. On the day of the funeral my father had arrived and, as always, he was little support. In truth, I would have hated it if he had actually said something kind or emotional or thoughtful to me, so we all just sat saying nothing of meaning, just being. For the funeral I wore a pair of velvet hot pants that my mother had made me. They were green and blue, the shade changed when the fabric was moved, they were really gorgeous and regrettably I lost them at a boy's house a few months later. Waiting in the hallway, my sister handed me a hanky which I rejected with disdain, as I was quite sure I would be keeping all tears and emotion in that day. The church where the funeral took place was just around the corner. My mother had been attending church quite regularly in the past couple of years. Possibly because she knew she was dying, and I suppose when we have this knowledge, we might begin to find guidance and support for our spirit. Other things in life point us here also, the death of a parent being one of them. She had hardly ever gone to church when we lived in Scotland and she seemed quite against the institution at times, but she had built up a relationship with the curate at the church as she had been there so much, so it was decided that he would lead the service. The church was and still is, a grand looking building with beautiful stained-glass windows and intricate wood carvings. You don't have to believe in God to appreciate a beautiful church. We walked and my father and my granny and perhaps my uncles went in the official car. In the church we all sat at the front and then they carried in my mother in a coffin. Having attended several funerals now, I understand this to be a usual occurrence, but my mother's funeral was the first I had attended, and I don't know what I had expected but it wasn't that her actual body would be there presented in front of us. A body in front of me, albeit covered in a coffin, distracted me and I don't remember anything that was said, but I do recall the sound of someone crying loudly behind me. All I could think was, be quiet. This sound is blocking out my ability to experience my own mother's funeral, can you just keep it down?

Eventually it ended and as I walked out, I walked past so many people that I hadn't realised were there. My friends' mothers from my old school in Scotland were there and I suddenly felt very aware of myself and my velvet hotpants. We went back to the house for the wake. Food and drinks, the usual. My father used to make sloe gin and a while back he had sent my mother a bottle. As much as they lived apart, they never really fell out and they remained close, perhaps even as lovers, I am unsure, but I do know that he never recovered from her death. Anyway, the sloe gin unbeknown to anyone else had been drunk by Emma and me some weeks ago and refilled with Ribena which is, as it happens, exactly the same shade as sloe gin. How convenient, we had thought at the time. When my father retrieved the bottle from the shelf and poured himself and others a glass, my heart dropped to the floor, and I disappeared upstairs.

One night after my mother's death I had seen that boy who I had previously been so obsessed with. I had given up on him as a boyfriend by this time and I hadn't actually seen him for weeks given my mother's death and all. I was quite indifferent about him which he obviously noticed, and he became more attentive than I had ever seen him. How strange. I was knew he was not for me, I had other things on my mind, I had been changed, so I didn't really entertain his uncharacteristic affection although it tickled me at the time. In the night while in bed I heard a banging on my window which was upstairs by the way. He had actually climbed up the drainpipe and was there wanting to get in. My sister and her boyfreind were in bed. They had moved into my home permanently now and Jane was now my official guardian, all the other sisters had gone home. Kay, I can't remember where she was at the time, but she was still ill and still receiving no care I know that much.

He had dropped to the ground by the time I got to the window, and I went down and let him in. My sister heard, of course, and she came down furious asking what was going on. He was a charmer this boy, he apologised, told her some bullshit about being worried about me and said he promised he wouldn't stay long. She begrudgingly went back upstairs to bed not without giving us both a serious look. I was in trouble, getting the look, yet still this whole situation was out of my control, and I was uneasy. Was he really worried about me? Did he care after all, was this it, the start of an actual relationship with this wild crazy boy who I had lusted after for so long? No. That night he raped me right there in my sitting room with my sister upstairs. The brass neck of this boy, the arrogance, the disregard for me was so clearly apparent. I did see him after that from time to time in the company of others, but he never came near me again. I wonder if he felt regretful or ashamed and that was why. Here's an odd thing that happened about 20 years later. I read a public message on a social media site that he had written. In this post he talked about being raped when he was seventeen and how he never recovered. I knew from the grapevine that he had indeed been in and out of mental hospital and he had been in prison also, for what I don't know, so this was possibly what he was referring to. He was a lot older than seventeen when he raped me. I wasn't sure if I now felt sorry for him or if I now felt even more violated. The uncomfortable truth is that even 20 years on I knew I was meant to feel something, but I actually felt nothing. I feel nothing now and I felt nothing then. That night he left, and I went upstairs and got into bed and went to sleep. I did not sob into my pillow or fail to function in the days that followed, I just do not recall thinking very much of it at all. Think. That is the key word here. My brain tucked that delightful incident right inside with all the other sorrowful events but my cells, my body, they took it in, and they felt it and my subconscious, it took note.

CHAPTER TWELVE

Despite having my nose put out by two new adults invading my space and my routine and my freedom, it was good for me to have their support in the home. They did ensure that I had food each day, made my tea, made sure there were things like toothpaste in the house and other basics which had been a bit haphazard as my mother had been out of action. My mother had just died, I was only 15 years old, I did need some care and we got used to each other after a while. It was an effort, but Jane was kind to me and even though I told myself I hated that, and I didn't need anyone, it was nice, and I didn't appreciate it as much as I should have. I missed her, you see, my mother, and while I wasn't allowed or given the opportunities to convey this to anyone by my carers and by myself, I felt it and a heavy, immense pain sat in my body.

Me being me, I sought out another avenue for release. I remembered what my mother had told me about astral travel and one evening as I sat with this heavy pain, I thought I'd give it a go, and go and get her, or see her at least. So, one day I lay down on my bed and, just as my mother had described, I said to myself, let's give this a go, and I imagined myself lifting from my physical body. To my utter shock, it worked. I felt it, like a tingling feeling in my feet at first as the two entities attached from each other and up I went and down I looked at my body there on the bed. I went up around the room to the ceiling and then I thought to myself, I need to get out. I went to the window and tried to open it, without my body I couldn't move the handle, but perhaps I didn't need to open it, perhaps I could go straight through the window? It was at this moment that I got afraid and just like that I was back in my body. I was fascinated and wanted more and more. I was searching, you see, for my mother. Where she had failed, I would succeed. I would try it out as often as I could, usually at night when I had gone to bed, but I could never get further than the window, something was stopping me, until one day it didn't. I was at my father's as it happened, I can't remember why and by this time it was out of control. As soon as I lay down, I was off, with no intent or effort at all, and on this occasion, I just kept going, up and up and up at such speed I don't know what I passed on the way and all of a sudden, I was in another place. That's all I can describe it as, and I knew I was not meant to be there. It wasn't people in the earthly sense with faces and bodies and clothes even that I saw, more like I knew they were people,

I couldn't see them fully, but they were rushing past me, this way and that. One after the other on and on they came from every direction, and I was scared. Get back, go back down, I told myself. You are not meant to be here! But I couldn't move. Shit shit shit, I've gone too far, I'm dead. That's what I honestly thought, and I didn't want to be, and I don't think I was. This is an odd tale, but this is how it happened, so make of it what you will. I used every part of my body, my soul, my energy to move myself back. I heaved and heaved and as I did the pain in my chest was unmeasurable. After what seemed like hours upon hours I was back. My entire physical body was wet with sweat, and I remember lying there in the dark, eyes wide open and I felt so exhausted that I thought I would never feel the need to move from that spot again. That was the end, it never happened again and like my mother, I never found who I was looking for.

I have in my life attempted to describe the events that transpired from this to a few different people, but I always felt unable to offer any kind of explanation, but I couldn't, because I had no idea what it meant. Life and the people I have met along the way have led me to a couple of conclusions. One is that the sheer gargantuan amount of energy running through my system forced my soul right out of my body and into places it wasn't meant to be. My will, my sorrow my desperation made this possible. The other is that this was my gift opening up to me, that I could communicate, engage, whatever you want to call it, with spirit, with the afterlife, the place where souls go when they no longer have a body on earth. The experiences were terrifying, so I stopped them, I shut that door, but of late I do hear whispers and my soul does travel a little.

CHAPTER THIRTEEN

All my encounters with boys up until I was 16, had been from a pool of males who were either from school or associates from people at school and it was not until then that I met a boy, Sam, who was completely unrelated to that scene, of smoking cannabis, drinking in the park, going to nightclubs, taking acid and whatever else. He was a good boy, and I was a bad girl, but when I met him I discovered I was quite open to the idea of not taking drugs and doing good things such as a date night at the cinema, in contrast to the stressful nights out late at night, never having quite enough money to get home or not knowing exactly where I was staying or with whom.

He was not ideal, not that attentive or kind but not unkind, and for me that was a step up, so that is what I was content to have as a boyfriend. The fact that he wanted to actually be my boyfriend seemed amazing to 16-year-old me. Nobody had ever wanted to commit to that with me before, so I ignored the flaws and we dated. We started to have sex inevitably, but this was very shameful I had been led to believe, so when he made no attempt to offer any discussion around contraception, I was unable to either.

How could I tell anyone, even a doctor, of this shameful activity I was partaking in on a regular basis. This is how much it had been impressed upon me that having sex was the most revolting act you could ever take part in and that in doing so I must in turn be the most revolting person to walk the earth. But biology is what it is, and before long I was having a baby.

This had to come out, of course, because before too long a baby would arrive and I couldn't keep that up my jumper forever. I wrote Jane a note to tell her. My inability to communicate how I felt and the way I had been unheard for so many years rendered me mute when it came to expressing my feelings. It still does sometimes. Note writing has been something I have used as a coping mechanism for this. It serves a purpose, it works, its fine. She didn't want to write notes to each other, so we talked and as excruciating as it was, I was relieved to find her in a kind and understanding frame of mind.

At the time, nobody in the family gave two shits about me after my mother had died. They rang and asked about Kay who did seem in a worse state than me but, still, I was a very young person and feelings of abandonment were setting firmly in my soul. Feelings that I was bad, was unwanted, unliked, all fuelled and enlarged with each day that passed and nobody spoke to me, checked in on me. Nobody except Jane, and I am quite sure she has no idea how much I attached myself to her. I fought against it, I fought with her directly even, but my soul, my young person in need firmly attached to her. So, when she left Newcastle to start a new life in Edinburgh when my little boy was about three, I was crushed. Abandoned. All true, my mind confirmed. You are not wanted, not loved, not worth it. She said she could see that I was fine and settled now so she could now go off and do what she wanted. From her point of view, at the age of 25 she had been landed with the responsibility of caring for a 15-year-old kid who brought a whole heap of drama to her life, who couldn't even go to school and act normally, who went off and got herself pregnant and who was now living in a shitty council flat with three GCSEs. I'd run away the first chance I got too, and she didn't know that I'd tied myself around her.

Jane told my father for which I will be eternally grateful. She said to me, the worst thing for him will be having to acknowledge that his child has had sex, but he will get over it. Cue another dose of disappointment in the bank for my father. First, I was a girl, then I was stupid, now he knew that I had had sex. Disgusting. He didn't say anything directly to me about this, he just ignored me for a few months.

CHAPTER FOURTEEN

My baby boy was born on November 15th at 11pm, just as the credits of *Prisoner: Cell Block H* were rolling on the telly. Baby Jake was here. When I became pregnant my baby suddenly became my focus. Emma wanted me to come over, to still do the things I had done just one month earlier, but I could not. I was no longer interested in drinking, in smoking or going to the pub, I was no longer going to be naughty, I was going to be good and be a good mother. Good mothers didn't do that sort of thing. Me and Emma did drift apart over the early years of Jake's life, but never forever and to this day she is still my oldest and dearest friend. Despite me insisting that I was only interested in being good and none of those frivolous things like deciding what to wear on a Saturday night were of any interest to me at all any more, my heart sank each time she told me an exciting tale from the night before on the phone, and even more when she announced that she and all the other girls from school were off on a girls holiday to Spain. Emma and I had talked so much about going away without our families on a wild girls' holiday. We had scanned endless holiday brochures, working out how much money we would need to do this, planning our wardrobes from the

Freeman's catalogue, thinking about mini travel shampoos and cocktails on the beach. How could she be going without me; she never even asked me if I wanted to go. I had to sit and look at the photos and pretend to love them, and ooh and ahh at the beach snaps and the photo of their room and laugh as I listened to all the outrageous stories of what went on. Left behind again, but this was my choice. I had decided to be bad and have unprotected sex and have a baby, so I was not allowed to share any of these feelings and words. If you get feelings, you stay quiet and sit right there because this was all your own fault so just you get on with it and remember, you can't ask for help. You said you could do this so nobody is interested in helping you. Your mess, not theirs.

I went into labour with baby Jake, my beautiful boy, six days after his due date and the labour was quite invasive. I was managing quite well, no real pain, yet *they* decided, I imagine because of my age, to fill me with drugs that I hadn't asked for. So many drugs that it stopped my labour, so I had to be given more drugs and needless to say my poor baby child was in quite a drugged state when he was eventually born. Why did they do that to me? I feel aggrieved for my younger self writing this. She didn't know what was supposed to be happening, she didn't ask for that yet that's what she got. It isn't the worst birth horror story I have heard but it doesn't make it any more excusable all the same. Ah well, just another violation, who's counting? I looked at this baby and it suddenly hit me that I had no clue how to look after him. I had never done this before, oh shit oh shit what have I done, I asked myself. In those days, babies were taken to the nursey on the first night so you can get some rest. Nice in theory but having just had your baby and then being told to shower, get into bed, and have your baby taken from you while you supposedly sleep is draconian. I didn't have the capacity to question this. I just waited for them to bring him back and I'd say that over the next 5 days, which is how long you stayed in hospital back then, I got the hang of it. I breastfed him, much to the distain of Sam's family who firmly believed bottle was best, I learned how to bath him, to get his clothes on without breaking his arms which seemed like a real possibility, and, you know, over the next couple of years of his life I muddled through. Jane was still there but this was when I made my fatal mistake. I was so hellbent on being good, as good as I could be, to prove I was not this ball of disgusting failure who committed this unforgivable crime of having a baby, that I refused to let her help. I hid any aspect of weakness. I was crushing it as a mother, I had no use for her, for anyone at all. Try and help me at your peril because I will shoo you away. She concluded that I did not need her, and she was free to go, and I lost her. This is not to say that she never helped me again because she did. As Jake got older, we would go up to her house for a week in the holidays and they would take him on little holidays from time to time, which was glorious, but that everyday support, just someone to make you a cuppa or who you can ring if you need to moan about how you've had no sleep for days. I never had that. Sam lost interest quite quickly in having a baby. He said he wasn't really keen on going to the park. Pushing a swing isn't my idea of an exciting life either pal, I used to think, but who else is going to do it? When Jake was a baby, Kay was periodically an inpatient at St. Nick's, the local psychiatric hospital. Emma had worked in the kitchens there as a teenager and she told me this awful story about a ward full of old women who had been there for almost their whole lives after having postnatal depression. They had been locked in and never got out. The smell of that hospital will never leave my memory. It wasn't like a normal hospital that smells clean and of disinfectant, no, it smelled like school dinners and tobacco, and sweat. Kay had eventually received some psychiatric care after she had been found walking down the middle of the road into oncoming traffic in nothing but a suit jacket and a pair of Doc Marten's. Schizophrenia was the diagnosis, likely triggered by taking a large amount of acid . She did act very strangely, it is true, and it was uncomfortable to be around her. She would tap on objects, open and shut doors, and say strange things. Shave her hair, write on the walls. I wasn't happy about her being locked away. I felt sorry for all the times I had been annoyed at her and I didn't want her to be ill. Selfishly, at the time I still needed her to be the Ellie who looked after me and helped me and the only person I could ask for help because she understood and never made me feel judged. Despite the cavernous entity of her mental health disorder, she remained my person. With no available friends, no other family in Newcastle, she had to be. Sam's family were very different, and I am not quite sure they understood me either. They had a very what you might call normal life. On a Sunday they ate a roast dinner, on a Friday it was fish. On Friday night they went to the club and their other pastimes were reading the paper or watching telly. That's a perfectly reasonable life to live but if I spoke about other things, like going to college or indeed breastfeeding, I felt like they looked at me and saw three heads. Here's the thing, despite this early rocky start we have remained in touch. They come to every family event I have; I go to every event they have. I sat with Sam's mother while his sister, gave birth to her 3rd child, and you know, it was ok! His sister understands a lot of the difficulties I have been through. She knows some of the things most other people never did and I can trust her which makes me feel huge gratitude for our relationship. It is a strong reminder that family is not necessarily a biological factor, that we can cocreate a family just as we are an integral part of creating our life.

Kay was in hospital periodically. In and out. In when she stopped taking her medication and out when they had forcibly injected it for a period of weeks, and she was stable again. While 'in' there would be the period where she was given more freedom and allowed out if accompanied, for walks down to the shops. I would act as her chaperone so, along with baby Jake, I would get the bus to St. Nick's and take Kay out. As he got older, he would ask me why she was in hospital, and I had told him at the time that her head hurt. I hadn't the knowledge to explain but I bet her head did hurt, so it wasn't too far from the reality. We would go for cuppas at the café with aunty Kay and Jake never cared or noticed her obvious quirks. As a young person I cared quite desperately about what people thought of me, and I would get embarrassed about being out with Kay at times. She would talk to anyone and say embarrassing things which she couldn't help and nor should she have had to. How freeing in a way to be in a place where you give zero shits about what you say and who to, I often thought, and a part of me wished I could be more like her.

Being a parent to Jake consumed my life as it should do, but I did little else, and I was bored a lot of the time. He was an energetic child, and I remember he would wake up at 5:30 am each day, and we would be cutting and sticking by 5:35am. As bright as a button might be something you'd say about him. He loved to chat and to look at fact books and he would remember the facts too. He was a big healthy boy, breastfed and fed on home cooked food and nurtured, I hope, as a young child. Sam and I weren't in any sort of employment. Shameful dolewallers. I had never had a job; I had no clue how to get a job and who would look after Jake? But Sam went to college, so while he was on the way to getting a job, we still didn't have any money. In 1993, if you were on the dole, you had barely enough to live on. I sat and planned out the meals for the two weeks we had money for. Very rarely did this include any treats like a chocolate biscuit. A pack of custard creams at Kwik Save was 22p, so that was affordable. Fuel bills, water rates and the phone bill were paid and after that we had not a thing. I remember that I had saved £5 once in the hope that I could go out for a drink with Emma. It had all been arranged but I had to spend it on something for Jake and so I cancelled at the last minute. Emma had been really annoyed with me, I remember she came round to my house, and she said to me, I've told everyone you are coming out now and they are expecting you and I'll look like an idiot. I said to her that I had had £5 but now I hadn't. She said to me, well that was no good anyway, where was £5 going to get you? Oh, my goodness, I felt low that day, but not as low as the day my beautiful little boy ran up to the letter box in excitement as the postman popped the letters through shouting,

"Hooray, the giro is here!"

My determined spirit kicked in. I am not living like this anymore, I thought to myself, and when that happens and an idea appears in my head, change will happen. This might not always be a great idea, or indeed a well thought out idea, but nevertheless this is what I tend to do. Jake was 3 years old, and I had become increasingly tired of Sam's lacklustre attempts at helping me parent. He sat day in day out in his little room, smoking rollies, doing his work and he never really came out until me and Jake went to bed. We had married the year before, really because I thought it's what we should do, not because it was what I had always dreamed of. I was truly intending to stay good and do it all correctly. Next, Sam would get a job and maybe we would even have another baby! I had in my mind how this would all work. I'd lost my family, but I would create my own. One that would be mine, wouldn't go off and die, stop speaking to me or run away and move to another city to get away from me. But it just wasn't right. My soul gave me a little nudge. Not right, let's move.

Jake and I moved to a flat in the next estate. I had no furniture but was given some beds and a cooker by the council. I wasn't allowed a fridge because that wasn't classed as a necessity unless I had to keep medication in it, so I bought a little cool box that I kept my milk and butter in, but it wasn't greatly effective. Well, this is all your own fault so you mustn't even think about feeling sorry for yourself, I said in my mind. Look, I did feel a bit sorry for myself, I did. I felt sorry that I had tried to get it right and now I was sitting even more alone than I was before. I got more money to live on from the government than as a couple, so this was a bit of a novelty. The giro still arrived at the door. Yes, I had left my husband but the next part of

GET UP

the get out plan had not yet fallen into place.

One day an unexpected giro arrived for £75. I felt the way you might expect if a cheque for £10,000 dropped on your mat. When I think about the practice of gratitude, I always say it changes depending on your circumstance. It has to. An unexpected £75 was like a lottery win that day and the gratitude I felt was different to the gratitude I may have felt when I was earning a large wage and perhaps received a £75 tax refund. That would be really nice, and I'd be very grateful but not with the same intensity. Jake and I got on the bus and went to town with this phenomenal amount of money in my purse and I bought him blue paint, a duvet, pillow and new duvet covers. Oh, the luxury. They were blue with white stars and spaceships on them, and I was excited to make him a nice bedroom in our new home which had some dubious wall coverings. In the sitting room, which incidentally I never used because of the lack of furniture, was painted dark blue with gold spraypainted swirls on it. There was the kitchen which was passable and the staircase which again was painted in a dark gloomy colour. I had painted the bathroom and the toilet a bright turquoise which cheered them up and I made a little blind with a pale coloured tea towel, I had painted a whale on it and hung it with a curtain wire across the little window. My room was the worst, painted a dark burgundy with the same spraypainted swirls. It occurred to me that the room resembled what I imagined a really down-market brothel to look like. Perhaps it had been one, it would not have surprised me. I got some cheap white paint to try and get rid of it, but it never covered it completely. The phrase 'you can't polish a turd' comes to mind when I think of some of the rundown places I have moved into over the years. I think you actually can, or at least you can pop a bit of paint on it, and it shines it up a tad.

When we came home another letter was waiting for me. You are being visited by a government officer to talk about your current benefit claim. My heart stopped. They knew. I knew. I knew this £75 had been a mistake and I wasn't entitled to it, and I knew that when I cashed it in and spent it, and now I was going to prison for fraud. I ran, full of adrenaline, to the phone box with Jake, to ring them. Perhaps if I found out what this was all about, I could save myself, prepare for jail in some way. They were shut, it was past five and I couldn't do a thing. I went back to the house, anxiety pounding in my body and, to my horror, realised I had left my bag with my purse in it, which still contained a large proportion of the £75, inside the phone box. I panicked so much I dragged Jake running back to the spot. He couldn't keep up and then on top of everything he fell, and he actually really hurt himself. One of those falls on a child's knee where there is a deep graze, blood, tears, the whole lot, but I had to just drag him up and carry on, that's how terrified I was about losing the money. I fully neglected my child's need to be lifted up and cared for after his fall and kept on running. The phone box was a good 10-minute walk away and it felt like one of those dreams where you run and run but you don't move. I tell you, when I reached that phone box and saw that bag was still there, purse and all, I have never felt such deep relief. That's what you call gratitude.

There were other times I left my bag behind. Like the time my boyfriend asked me to 'keep hold' of £3,000 for him and I left it in my bag at the soft play. I was grateful that I got that back because my life literally depended on it. Or the time I left my bag at the side of a river out with the kids. In it were my car keys and my purse. Luckily, I got that back too. The time I left my bag at a restaurant when we were on holiday in Alicante, which again contained all our euros for the trip plus the key to the hotel room, and my bank card. Was this stress or something else?

Another bonus of being a single parent was that Jake would

go and stay with his dad once a week, so I totally took this opportunity to go out and have a bit of fun. I was still only 21 years old. Side note: It's disgusting really that the only time my child's father cared for his son while I took a break was when we were separated. Not when we were in a supposedly supportive partnership.

When Jake was still little, I met a woman, another mother at playgroup. I can't even write her name, so let's refer to her as M. She captured me. I am not sure how else to describe it, and it wasn't until I spoke to a counsellor about it aged 40 that I realised that what had happened to me was grooming. It wasn't until I wrote this book that I realised how traumatising it had been.

We had chatted, as you did at drop offs and pickups, but she was at least 10 years older than me. When I left Andrew all the other mothers had quite surprisingly been in awe of me. These older women shared with me the stories of their useless husbands who hit them and didn't help look after their kids either, and I felt a bit like a spoilt brat if I am honest. Yes, my husband was totally absent from our life, but he didn't hit me. Perhaps I had read this all wrong but nonetheless I enjoyed the legend status I now had at the playgroup. The thing was, I was now a young single mother, and I might lure their abusive cheating husbands away from them, so most of them kept their distance, but not M, in fact, she wanted to be with me all the time. She groomed me and so did her husband and I didn't even notice.

I was a free woman without caring responsibilities for one night a week at least and I could have been out with Emma, or making new friends, perhaps meeting a nice boy, dating, being good, yet somehow all my free nights started to be spent at her house drinking cheap wine with her and her four kids and her husband. Each time I attempted to do something that wasn't spending my time with her, she stopped me and in time I didn't even try. It was how it was, and I had no way out of it. I didn't have the words and in time I didn't have the will either, because this was ok, fun even. We drank wine and had a laugh? All her husband's friends really liked me, they seemed to laugh at my jokes and be happy I was around. This was good, wasn't it? It was what I wanted, to have people around me who liked me and accepted me. My time with them leaked into my time with Jake.

"Bring the bairn down, I'll pop the pool in the garden they can all play," and of course Jake had a ball rolling around with all the kids and my capacity to say no and stick to what I wanted, such as taking my child home to eat his tea and put him to bed like a good mother, started to go away. I could not get out of it. I could not say no thankyou when she asked me to visit, and I could not leave when I wanted to. I still find it hard to say no. People who have not experienced abuse will often say,

>"You just leave. One foot in front of the other and you walk away. You just say no."

I'm sorry, but that is just not possible.

Her house stank. The kids all wet the bed and they had a smelly dog. She shouted and swore at her kids and her house was very unsafe. She told me about how her husband had abused her, hit her, had once hung her on the washing line and her neighbours had thought she was a blow-up doll. I was scared of him because of what she told me, yet I never saw him do this to her, and they seemed very close and loving towards each other when I was with them. I do believe that what she told me was true, but I do believe they wanted to keep me happy and not to scare me away, so this is how they pretended to be.

The first time they set me up was with this man's cousin.

We were to go out for the night, and she had told me he was a really good-looking boy. At this time, I was 21 years old. He was not a good-looking boy, and I don't want to talk ill of anyone because of their looks but let's just say I was not attracted to him. The thing is, I was taken out by these people to the pub with this boy, bought a load of drinks and the next day I had somehow had sex with him, and he was now my boyfriend. Writing this, I know how it must sound. Every part of me was unable to stand up for myself. My body, my mind, my voice. He remained my boyfriend until I became pregnant and something in me knew that being attached to this man and his family was dangerous. My flight response kicked in so fearfully I ended the relationship and had an abortion. I didn't get the care and support I needed with this, like so many women across the world in desperate situations. I made the mistake of telling M and she warned me his family would kill me if they found out and I was very scared. Lucky me, she would protect me, she would keep my secret. How grateful was I going to have to be to her now?

The abortion experience was horrific. When I went to arrange the procedure, the consultant said to me,

>"Did you know that this procedure puts you at risk

of never having a baby again, is this what you want, never to be able to have children ever again?"

I had to answer 'yes,' it didn't fully seem like something I wanted to say yes to, but I had no other option than to say yes. Yes, meant possible assassination, however, so yes was still a shitty option.

When I woke up in the bed after the procedure a nurse came over me and said,

> "Your baby was a girl by the way, just in case you wanted to know."

Then she left, and I sat feeling like a disgusting naughty little girl.

In the months after that, I shopped for baby clothes. Not many, only because I didn't have the finances. I bought a set of vests, one white, one pink and white stiped and one white with pale pink rabbits on. A set of pink dummies in a little clear box. I used to sit and fold them and unfold them and open the little clear box and look at the dummies. I had them in a big bag, the sort you put gifts in which read 'New Baby Girl' on the side.

One night M and her husband asked me to babysit while

they went out. I was more or less their live-in nanny, cleaner and cook by this time. Jake was with me; he and the other kids were asleep in bed when a man – T – walked through the door, a friend of the husband who I had met before but had not been expecting to visit.

"They're not in" I said as he simply walked into the house.

"I know," he said, "they told me you would be here".

I was 22 years old. This man was 35. He had an ex-wife whom I later discovered he would still visit and sleep with regularly, so goodness knows what she was having to deal with. He officially lived with his mother who was a Jehovah's Witness but also a member of the National Front and an alcoholic.

I was not attracted to this man. He was not aesthetically pleasing to me. He was being very nice and kind to me, though, and I reluctantly made him a drink and we talked for a while. He was interested in what I had to say. He said to me,

"You seem older than 22, you're wise."

I was not wise. Not wise at all. Here I was again, mother, in a house alone with a man unable to control this situation and out of my depth. This man proceeded to have sex with me, but I did not want to have sex with him. I did not enjoy the sex, but I did not care too much about it either. After all, he had all the power, I had none, and this was just what I had begun to accept as my lot. I think this possibly protected me in some way. Perhaps my mind shutting it all off was the only possible way to survive and put one foot in front of the other each day. After we had sex, he asked me,

> "Why did you just let me have sex with you, have you no respect for yourself?"

I was embarrassed, I remember that, and I said to him,

> "It was what was expected of me."

He laughed so hard at me when I said that.

> "You should make a man wait for you, make him honour you and love you and care for you, not just have sex with anyone who you think might expect it."

It was clear in my head now what I was. A slag, a disgusting whore who just had sex with anyone, who had no respect for herself. He had it set in his mind that I was fair game. I was definitely someone who he could abuse, no question about it, he had me now.

Don't you laugh at her, she is Silvia! Beautiful, funny, talented Silvia who can do anything she puts her mind to. Amazing mother to this glorious clever child who will achieve all his life goals and live a happy and fulfilling life and she does not need you to come along and laugh at her and make her feel small. You will not spend the next 4 years breaking her into tiny pieces, you leave her alone!

He did not leave me alone and he too began to groom me. I had no money so he would buy me nice food and take Jake and I out in his car to the beach, to the countryside. Things I loved to do, but I lived in a vast council estate nowhere near these places with no means of getting there so when he took us, I had to feel gratitude. This is where I really learned that people don't offer things for free. I had to unlearn this of course because they do but, in this life, they didn't. There comes a time when they want a repayment. I was trapped into doing whatever this man asked of me because I owed him. What he did to me over the period of our 'relationship' made me question everything about myself. By the end of it I was very unclear about what I thought and how I felt about anything, and my default became to feel nothing at all.

CHAPTER FIFTEEN

Because the events that followed between the age of 22 and 27 were so traumatic, I found it difficult to recall when and how events had happened when I first spoke about this to my counsellor. It was all a sort of muddle which I think is part of the reason I never felt able to tell anyone. I was usually of the mindset that whatever had happened was my own fault, so how could I complain with any conviction?

With the counsellor I worked on a timeline in a bid to put it all in some sort of order. I was telling her that I had become increasingly anxious within my current relationship and in particular I was finding the actions of my husband so unbelievably unbearable I couldn't think, to the point where I wanted to scream. This may or may not sound strange to you depending upon your own life experiences, but it was the noise he made. He had a habit of coming in from work and emptying the dishwasher. How helpful you might think, and yes, emptying the dishwasher is great but it made me recoil inside and it was distressing because I had no idea why. It became more, it grew in my mind and fear attached itself to this simple act. I was worried, was he angry that I had failed to empty the dishwasher so as he did the job, I became afraid. He never shouted, he never said anything, but I felt his anger was expressed in ferocity that the plates were clattered out of the drawers and into the cupboards. I wanted to shout, 'Just leave it!' but I could not.

I had to be grateful that he was doing this for me because I had failed. I sat there each day, heart pounding, rigid, unable to move, just listening to the sound which was so loud in my head. Even though he never once shouted at me regarding the dishwasher, never hit me for being so useless, I was terrified none the less. How could I express this to him? It sounded to me like he was standing on a chair and harpooning each and every spoon and fork and knife into the cutlery drawer. If I offered any criticism about the way he was emptying this dishwasher it was as if I was saying that I wasn't grateful for his help. One day I just couldn't stand it anymore and I had to speak, and of course he was angry then. Why didn't you keep your mouth shut, you stupid woman, I thought, now look what you have done. He does think you are ungrateful; he does think you are criticising him and he does think you are pathetic. The outcome was that he refused to modify the sound. I told him it upset me, and he refused to make any allowances for that. This was the alarm. Looking back, I can accept that he would struggle to fully understand the impact this action was having upon me. Regardless, he wouldn't change.

The counsellor asked me if anything else made me feel this fear. Yes. Each time he opens the door when he returns from work. Each and every time I heard this noise, I feel this fear. I hear the door and I freeze, and I wait as I do an assessment of the situation. I listen intently for any more information that can tell me if I am safe or if I need to take action to protect myself. The fact that, despite the frustrated emptying of the dishwasher, nothing ever did happen made no difference to how I felt. She said to me, I think you have PTSD. PTSD? The thing that soldiers get when they have fought in a war. I had a sudden memory. After the final catastrophic event that happened to me at the hands of T, I had gone to the doctors. I had been awake for 2 days straight and I was worried and really tired, and I thought perhaps they would give me some sleeping tablets. I didn't want to talk about my feelings, but my face was black and blue, so she had a fair idea that something bad had happened. I told her that I had seen a pool of blood on the side of my bed, and I had been sick. She said to me,

"You have PTSD."

She gave me some sleeping tablets, which didn't work I

hasten to add, and that was it. This infuriates me now that I have a better understanding of the way brains work. Had I had some support at this time to process what had happened this would have given me a higher possibility of recovering. That's not an opinion, it's science. I didn't have any support and I carried on with PTSD through another 13 years, another 2 marriages and the death of my father, to name a few things that fed my fear and anxiety, so by age 40 I was full. My mind and my body were in absolute crisis, and it was all spilling out all over the place in some pretty crazy and erratic ways. Having a breakdown over the noise of a fork going into a drawer being one of them.

CHAPTER SIXTEEN

T took it upon himself to be the saviour. I was a piece of lowlife shit who didn't discipline her child properly and he would educate me because he was better than me. Jake was a wild, creative child but also very sensitive and loving and before this point me and him had got along just fine. T put it into my head that I was doing this all wrong and if I did not fall into line, I would have a 10-year-old swearing at me and telling me what to do like all the other radgie kids on the estate. Being a good mother was something I hadn't actually questioned before, because I was pretty sure before I met him that I was doing ok at this one. Yes, I had moved us around a bit and this wasn't great and, yes, I had initiated the separation from my husband, my child's father, but these are not heinous crimes and throughout all of that I was still a kind and a loving mother and I spent time with my child and read to him and played with him and fed him and made sure he had shoes and clothes and all the things you would expect, even though this was often a real challenge. This was actually what he criticised me for. He somehow convinced me that what I was doing, the way I was caring for my child, was wrong and in fact I needed to do less. I needed to get him out on the street playing and not relying on his mother to play with, so because I was nothing and he was everything I believed him, and Jake began to play out in the street with the radgie kids whose mothers never spoke to me. They all viewed me as an outsider. I wasn't the same, I hadn't lived there my whole life, so I was not one of them. Just to add, that boy has never disrespected me as T said he would. He never lost his calm, kind and sensitive nature but Jake has a toughness that I am 100 percent sure was learned growing up on the streets of a Newcastle council estate. I learned to fight too. I argued with mothers if I had to. I argued with kids if I had to! This sounds cliche but it was dog eat dog. At this time, we had moved two streets away from M. She initiated the move. She told me I needed to be nearer her and nearer Jake's school so, as she had a good friendship with a man at the housing office, they pushed it through and got me a move right next to her.

T would criticise my clothing and the way I had my hair. He said that how I dressed and the makeup that I wore gave people the wrong impression and I should wear something more conservative, wear less makeup, even down to the underwear that I wore. He shamed me for my fun wonder woman knickers and pink bras and bought me large floral-patterned briefs and long nighties that he said were more appropriate. I went along with this because I wanted to be good, and if being good meant wearing old lady briefs then that was what I would do. But I was losing myself. I was unable to think for myself, this is what he was doing, making me incapable of free thought, or choosing what I wore, or choosing what I ate. At one point I did not even know what I liked to eat. Doesn't that sound strange? I was unable to decide for myself what flavours I enjoyed, and I took all my instructions from other people.

The only positive thing to happen from the relationship I had with T was that it saved me from M. By this time, I'd been subjected to numerous sexual assaults in their home, by others and by them both, but now I owed T because he had saved me from them. The fact that he exploited and sexually assaulted me too did not seem to be an issue, for me as well as him, and the longer it went on the harder it was to say anything, to him or to anyone else. There are things that he did to me that I still don't feel I will ever be able to share with another person, certainly not write in this book. Things that would make you sick, that have made me vomit and I don't think anyone would ever want to hear about them, it would not make enjoyable reading and for the purposes of telling my tale you know enough. Here I was, past questioning myself and now just in a space where what I thought or felt was of zero importance. My body was at the mercy of any request this man put upon it. And, just like that, T decided he no longer wanted to spend time with me. Just like that, he abandoned me. He took me apart, so I was no longer a person, and left. His wife had decided she would give him another chance it would seem, and I had been so insignificant to him that I could easily be discarded. You know all the strong women talk, you should kick him to the curb, he treated you bad why would you want him, he doesn't deserve you. All correct, yes, but when you have been kept captive in this way, by words, by fear, your brain attempts in some way to make the situations safe, so it decides to form positive feelings towards the very people who are abusing you. It's known as Stockholm Syndrome, you may have heard of it, and for the abused person, for me, it made me even more afraid. It made me even more disgusted in myself and ultimately more at risk. Ah that pesky brain of ours! As a hypnotherapist, I now love working with people and allowing them to realise that while a lot of what we do and feel seems illogical, it is a result of our brain attempting to keep us safe. It means therefore, without doubt, you are none of the awful things you say you are. What it means is that you are wired to survive and, look, here you are, right here today, so you did survive didn't you? Now, let's move on to living.

When a few weeks later T smashed in my windows because he was convinced I had met another man, I was strangely relieved to think he still cared about me. He did not. His wife had just changed her mind and now he wanted to come back to his plaything. The police had been called by a neighbour and the next day they rang me to ask if they could let him out. We have your boyfriend here. Not my boyfriend, I said immediately. He ignored me. We just want to check you are ok with us letting him out. I stumbled at this. Honestly, I wasn't. This man had abused me physically and mentally for the past two years and finally I was feeling slightly human again after he left me to go back to his wife. If there is an option for you to keep him in jail, like you seem to be saying, that I somehow I have some control over this then, no, I am not ok about you letting him out. So, I said to him 'no', and this was his reply.

"Well, we can't actually keep him in, I really just wanted to let you know we were letting him out with a warning, and we have told him not to come near you, unless you want to make any formal complaint against him."

At the time, I had no idea how to do this or what it would mean, and this bloke on the phone wasn't readily dishing out this information, but I was scared of this man to my core, and if the police had told him not to come near me again then this seemed like it was all sorted and I would be safe so I told them it was fine, I would be fine.

T assumed I had rung the police and for that I paid a hefty price. Broken ribs take an age to heal and there isn't a lot you can do about it. I still have a strange bump that I can feel under my skin where one of the breaks healed. It's as if my body put a little blanket around my wound to keep it safe or to help it heal. That's how I like to think of it anyway. After that he did go away for a while. Each day that passed and I didn't see him again, I relaxed a little more, but never fully. He was no longer fully present but guess who was? M. and she wasn't happy either that I had left her. She started what can only be described as a hate campaign against me. The truth does not come into it when you want to bring a person down. I wouldn't even know where to begin in piecing it all together. The stories that came back to me ranged from me being a prostitute to me being a drug dealer, to being a thief, a husband-stealer. My goodness, it was relentless. I had seen her do this to people before, people with more standing in the community than me so I knew I would never recover, no matter what I said. Can you imagine how it feels to come out of your house and feel afraid of every person that you see? An entire estate of people who had known each other their whole lives bonded together against me. The outsider, the single mother who was a slag, who had no friends, no family and nobody who would stand up for her and who certainly had no capacity to stand up for herself against this huge force. The victim.

Looking back, my mind at this point was in a seriously distressed state but, do you know, in the middle of this that poor young girl was still sticking to the plan. Remember the one where she left her husband who was no support, then she somehow made a great new life for her and her child? Education had been the one thing that I had been told would see you to this destination, so I had enrolled at college and was taking some A-levels, or whatever they were called at the time. Essays were handwritten back then so, luckily, I didn't need a computer or anything other than a pen and some paper. Thank goodness, as I didn't have the means to get anything else. Every single person in my family went to university because this was how you got a good job and a good life; this is what I had been conditioned to believe. At this point in my life, I am quite sure my entire family thought I was a lost cause and had no expectation of me going to university. They had not one idea of what I was living with and had gone through. I did visit them from time to time; my uncle in his enormous house in Edinburgh, my father at the farm, my granny in Berwick with her solid views on what makes a person good or bad, and when I did, I had to put on a show. I had to somehow convince them that I was deliriously happy in my cute little council flat, that being a mother was everything I hoped it would be, that I was making my wonderful plans to study and get a really well-paid job, and this was just a little blip. Smiles, laughter, cracking jokes, these were all great ways to convince those around me that I was absolutely fine, and I did not need any support at all. Just leave me be I am great thank you!

The strain and the fear of an entire estate wishing you harm was a lot to manage. I could not ask anyone for help. I could not at this point even begin to explain how this had happened, so I panicked and did something rash and impulsive, just for a change! These were not normal circumstances, my brain was under immense stress, so I went to the one person who I didn't have to hide from, who knew every dark and repulsive thing about me. I went to T. He relished in the fact that I had come back to him, and there he was, the knight in shining armour who would sort it all out for me, he would get me and Jake out of there, he would get my belongings, he would get me a new house and I would be grateful and owe him forever and ever and ever. In reality, I left my home, along with most of my belongings because I was so frightened of what these people would do to me. For a period of time Jake and I were homeless. This was a really awful time; it was cold to boot as we entered into winter. We stayed with T for a while, but his alcoholic mother did not want us. I didn't want to stay there either, but I didn't have many options. I went to Kay. She still lived in Newcastle and probably had the best idea of what I was going through but I still hid a lot from her, and when I visited her, I didn't want to spend time talking about the shit I had just left behind, I wanted a break! Kay still had a serious mental illness, and you know she had a lot of her own things to deal with, mainly her own abusive partner. Kay was my true protector; she was my big sister who had always helped me, so when I went to her and asked if me and Jake could stay with her and she said no, it was like a wrecking ball to the chest. Her partner had a flat though, and so he eventually said we could stay there, and he would stay with Kay. This was not an ideal plan. He was after all an abuser himself, and this meant putting her in a space where she couldn't escape from him, even if it was for a day when he went home to his flat. I was desperate, there are no two ways about it, and so I took him up on his offer despite knowing it was fully for his own gain, and I just hoped beyond hope that it wouldn't be for long. Thank the universe, the moon, the gods – you name it – in a short time a council house became available and I moved in on November 16th a day after Jake's 7th birthday. I had bought him a Bart Simpson cake and I was so sorry that when we moved, I forgot to take what was left out of the fridge and bring it with us. He was so upset that he had lost his cake. More than leaving the cake, I was sorry about all of this disruption for Jake. One day he was at his home and the next he wasn't, and he was living with a crazy drunk old woman with none of his belongings. He left all his friends because he couldn't go to the same school anymore and then we ended up living in a smelly flat where he and I shared a single bed, and while I found him a new school, we had to travel miles to get there on the bus each day. I had told the nice school that I was waiting on a house in the catchment area but, as yet, we didn't have an actual address and they judged us, Jake and I, as not good enough for their school and they told me they could not accept a child into their school with no address. This reaffirmed in my mind, you are scum. A school that I used to nickname Broadmoor accepted him, but after a few months in attendance, a few black eyes, and a serious lack of quality teaching, I took him out and we were on the move again. Sorry Jake.

How did T want to be repaid do you think? Sex, first and foremost, any time he desired it. He also wanted to be able to be in my home, the one he moved me into, the one he decorated even though I said I would manage myself, the one he fitted carpets in and sourced furniture for without me wanting him to, without me asking. The one he brought food to, unwanted food that I wasn't in need of. He was relentless and sometimes I fought back and sometimes I was too tired. He was still living on and off with his wife and with his mother, so his visits were sporadic. The way he really got me was when I had his baby. In all of this nonconsensual sex I had fallen pregnant. My brain was in such a state that I never even noticed until I started violently vomiting one day. This happened to be one day before my father was due to visit me. I knew I was pregnant, and I tried frantically to stop myself being sick, somehow if I got all of the sick out before he arrived that would work but it just wouldn't stop. I had a condition called hyperemesis, which essentially means you can't stop being sick and in time you suffer with severe dehydration and left unattended you can even die. When my father arrived, I was in bed, and I was so weak it was impossible to put on any kind of an act. I asked him to call a doctor and she came, and I had to tell her I was pregnant and then I had to tell my father. Despite all of the work I have done on myself and my self-worth, the shame and disgust I felt about myself is still present writing this. Filthy dirty girl I was. I was so unwell I was taken to hospital that day leaving my father to care for Jake. He didn't come to see me, I had no money, no clothes with me, no idea how my little boy was. A few days later, on Christmas Eve, I was released from hospital just having to hope my father was still at my house with my child. I got a taxi home, reassuring the driver I would pay him when we arrived, but that was a lie. My father was not home but just at that moment Lucy arrived. I have no idea why, or how, and I did not think to ask. It was as if an actual angel had driven up the road in her vintage van and saved me. She paid the taxi and we waited for my father as the door was locked and I had no key. I worried that they had gone completely. I wonder how long we would have waited, but soon after my father walked down the path. He barged straight past me, didn't look at me. He opened the door, went into the kitchen and opened his suitcase. He took out a letter and handed it to me then he walked out the door without a word. I ran after him and shouted,

"Where are you going?" but he didn't look back and walked on.

In the letter he told me as clear as day what he thought of me, and it was exactly what I had imagined. Disappointment, reckless, thoughtless, stupid, useless. I had brought nothing but shame and upset to everyone. The conclusion. Because of this final act, of extreme badness, of having a baby, I was no longer to contact him or my beloved Granny Katherine. If I tried, he would ignore me, so I was to leave them both alone. Cruel is the only word I can use now to describe what he did to me that day. I cried inconsolably. I didn't cry for years after my mother died; this was the first time since then that id cried like this.

I finished crying and then I had to get my shit together. I had to! It was Christmas Eve, I had not one gift for my child, not one bit of Christmas dinner in the cupboards, but so many moments of real relief, real life gratitude. Yes, we can all sit and be grateful for food in our bellies and a roof over our head. These moments, when an angel saves you, when you need something badly and it arrives, have a strength and impact that marks the very essence of you. I had been in such a mess over the previous few weeks and then so unwell that I hadn't spent any money. I hadn't paid any bills; I hadn't bought any food to speak of and so this meant that I had a whole bunch of money in my purse. Lucy drove us to the supermarket, the big one that sells everything including toys and Christmas PJs and I spent it all, every penny, on trying to salvage something that represented a happy day with food and toys for my little boy. All those gargantuan feelings about being pregnant, and my father disowning me, they just got tucked in and I did as I always did, I got up and I got on with it because I literally had no choice. Falling apart was not an option.

CHAPTER SEVENTEEN

One tiny bit of relief was that while I was pregnant T didn't rape me. Nice. Jake was visiting his father when Rowan arrived. Jane was staying with me when I went into labour and with me when Rowan was born. She was the very best person you could have at your side when having a baby. Practical, which is actually exactly what you need, and not a lot of fuss and pampering, because when you are in a lot of pain your brain goes a bit skew-whiff and instructions like 'Close your mouth when you push' were actually extremely helpful. And she was kind to me. She didn't say anything particularly poignant; she just didn't shout at me or criticise me. At the time, to me, that was kindness and comfort and so gratefully received. I wasn't even sure if I should ring T and tell him Rowan had been born. I was clear with him and had been for some time now that he was not my partner, I did not in any way wish to have a relationship with him. I felt like my words were clear, but I was in this horrific place where I said all this and then he would rape me, and if I didn't fight back, he took this as confirmation that I wanted him and I was back to square one. Exhausting is the only word to describe this. I did reluctantly ring him; his mother answered, and she was as enthusiastic about the news as I was as knowing my child was related to her. When he arrived at the hospital and he picked her up, a surge of emotion flew through me like a dragon. I didn't know it at the time, but this was my soul giving me a strong message. With all my might I needed him to put her down. I grabbed her back. He didn't really care about her, about holding her, so he didn't protest, and he left.

For the next 2 years this was how my life was. Me, Jake, and Rowan lived together in our house and Jake went to school and played out in the streets with the drug dealers' kids, learning how to be tough. In the evening he came home, and I read him Harry Potter in bed. Rowan and I went to the baby and toddler groups and after completing all my qualifications while I was pregnant, I applied to university. My route out of here. I didn't associate with any of my neighbours. I still saw Emma from time to time but not much at all, and I stayed safe away from anyone as much as I could. T continued to, what we would now call, stalk me. He would follow me, turn up at places he knew I would be, knock on my door wanting in at 7am in the morning so I couldn't pretend I was out, and of course rape me at every chance he got. I never realised this was rape. I was too tired and quite frankly too busy a lot of the time that my body had become completely disassociated from the sex. It had learned that very quicky it ended and then he would be more likely to go away. If I protested, he would stay longer or perhaps not go home at all. This was the worst because he would stop me from sleeping if he stayed, the way they do to torture people. To this day, if I need to sleep and there is a possibility that I may not be able to sleep it makes me very anxious. This was a difficult thing to manage when I had my third child. If I am asleep and someone wakes me abruptly, even by accident, it evokes in me a reaction that, if I were unable to control myself, would have me attack that person physically. I can control it but energy roars around me. Fear, upset, anger. It's very intense.

One particular incident has played over in my mind countless times. One day T decided to have sex with me, but this time I could not bear it and I tried to stop him. He punched me clean in the face, the sort of punch that leaves you dazed and disoriented for a while, and he pinned me down and had sex with me anyway. I kicked and screamed out of pure frustration and hatred for this man even though it would not stop him. Afterwards it was time to get Jake from school, so I was getting my bag and coat and such like, calm as you like, and he started laughing at me, mocking me, just as he had done back then at M's house.

"I've just raped you and you don't even seem bothered. What sort of a woman are you?" he said to me.

A one that has to get her child from school I thought, a one that has no option to fall apart, now fuck off.

CHAPTER EIGHTEEN

When Rowan had just turned two and Jake was away staying with my sister for a few days, an unbelievable opportunity arose for me to go out with my friend Cherry, and I went for it and asked the girl along the street if she could watch the baby for me. She was always asking, and I always said no, mainly because I was scared to go out, and by scared, I mean scared of what T would do to me if I dared to go out. This is just how it was, but that night I plucked up the courage and sorted it out. Safety was my primary concern. I needed to make sure the babysitter and Rowan were safe while I was gone. Writing this, it's as if I am writing about another person, just a side note, this part is tough going for me.

That day T had been at my house as usual but what I had worked out was that after he had sex, I was usually free for at least a day so, I had a great plan. If we had sex I would get a free window of time, so I actually initiated the sex. I needed to get it over and done with so he would be satisfied and go home, leaving me free to go out without fear that he would pop back round again later and find out I wasn't there. Bear in mind that I was not in a relationship with this man, but I often thought to myself that the only way this was ever going to end was if he died. I didn't ever contemplate murder, but I absolutely get why some women do. He was a very heavy drinker and often coughed up blood, so I had some hope that he might in fact be killing himself. How awful of my soul to think such a thing about another human, but that's where I was.

Despite having a great old time dancing and drinking in the wild town of Newcastle, I was conscious that I did have to get home. Cherry's brother had just been dumped by his girlfriend and wasn't really up for a night out, so when I said I was getting the bus home, he said he'd come with me. He hadn't known I had moved; it had been that long since I'd seen him, and when the bus we had hopped on started going the wrong way to his house he asked if he could come to mine and get a taxi. He was happy to see me home, we had a completely platonic relationship, he was my friend's little brother and I never looked at him as anything else. Why, pray tell me dear woman, are you still justifying yourself here? You were free to do whatever you wanted. In we came, and I tell you this because it's important for later, but he came in and he took his shoes off. I remember making a joke about it. You don't need to take care of my floors I've got a boy and a toddler. The babysitter went home, and he rang a taxi, and I probably made a cuppa, then it happened. There was banging at the door, and I just knew it was T. My thought process was this. T will think that me and Cherry's brother are here to have sex with each other. T will kill him and then he will kill me. I told this young and increasingly concerned young man to get upstairs and hide in Jake's room. I showed him where it was, and I went to see the baby. I heard a crash and then footsteps and I was terrified. Rowan was awake and I picked her up and held her into me. I didn't leave the room, I was frozen, but I heard T find that poor young man and I heard screams and crashing, doors slamming, more footsteps and it was quiet for a few moments. I stood there listening, still unable to move, then he walked in the room where I stood. At this point I was 100 percent sure there was a dead body at the bottom of my stairs and when he said to me

"I've killed him."

I was not surprised. He punched me in the face and the next thing I knew I was on the floor with Rowan still in my arms, he picked up a stool that I had and crashed it down upon me and it spilt into pieces. Very luckily the majority of the force had been taken by the side of my bed frame, which I was lying down next to, but at the time I thought it had hit my little girl. He dragged her from me and started to walk away. I ran after him and he kicked me to the floor, kicking my head, my side my whole body, but as he walked down the stairs I got up and followed him. Get up, get up! He went into the sitting room, the was floor covered in glass where he had broken in. Blood was all over the walls, I assumed from the murder that had just happened in my house. Just to let you know, Cherry's brother was not dead. He was injured but he was alive, and he had run away, no shoes on his feet though because they were still at my front door. T still had Rowan in his arms. She was 2 years old, she said not a word and she did not move. He got a stanley knife out of his pocket. He often had such a thing in his pocket as he was a hunter, which incidentally saved him later on in this case, and he held it to her neck.

"Tell me you were shagging that boy, or she dies."

"It's Cherry's little brother," I said.

The look on his face told me he hadn't realised, but he continued.

"Tell me or she dies."

"Ok" I said, "Yes that's it that's what was

happening, now give her back".

Of course, I said it. He walked out of the house with Rowan, and I ran after her.

"Follow me and she dies" he said.

And calm as anything, he walked up the path away from the house and I had to watch. It seemed like a million years that I stood there. Time stopped. Then he just brought her back. A moment of redemption perhaps? I will never know. But when he brought her back, he said to me,

"Call the police."

I followed his instruction but as they answered the phone, he left. I haven't a clue what I said to them but in a short while police and an ambulance arrived at my house. Rowan and I were sitting on a wooden chair in the kitchen. She was on my knee in her little red nighty with *101 Dalmatians* on it. She loved that nighty, and she never got it back because the police later took it as evidence. She was wet with blood, her hair, her little face too but me and the police officer checked every inch of her, she was not injured. The blood had come from him. Gratitude, once again. Another call from a house about 10 minutes away had been made to the police. His wife. He had turned up there and told her he had killed somebody, and he had gone back home to his mother's house and waited for the police to arrive. Rowan and I went in the ambulance to A & E. When I arrived, the first person I saw was Cherry's brother. He was there with his friend, Keith, who I recognised as a parent from the school. The two of them went with me into the hospital, and I was both relieved and confused to see him alive. He was overwhelmed with guilt at leaving me. I told him not to be. I needed the toilet, and it was strange, I remember that this normal everyday occurrence was still happening amidst this chaos. Rowan sat with the two men, and I went to the bathroom. This is when I saw my own face. Covered with blood, misshapen, not my own. Unbelievably I had not one broken bone or fracture, so I was discharged. Yet again at a hospital with no money and a child in a nighty, wet with blood, late at night. Keith had driven them to the hospital because this is where he had gone when he ran from my house, so Keith drove me too, back to his house where his girlfriend found me some clothes for Rowan, and they lent me a buggy to put her in. Angels. Me and Rowan left their house in the early hours of the morning. The thought of going home seemed unsafe but there was nowhere else to go, so we walked home. The birds were singing, it was getting lighter, and I was suddenly very conscious of how I looked, and I practically ran home so I wouldn't be seen.

T was arrested and charged with aggravated burglary but, get this, when he told them, quite truthfully that earlier that day I had initiated sex with him, and that he regularly stayed at my home, still true technically, he claimed he had been led to believe, by me, a terrible sexual predator, slag of all time, mother of his daughter – me – that we were in a relationship, so when he saw me returning home after a night out with another man, this had driven him to do what he had done. Stupid Silvia, who had never shared with another human being what had been happening to her, never made a complaint to the police, never told a soul she had been raped and abused for years now, had not one leg to stand on. That's how I felt, and that's how the police made me feel. They said to me that if I took this to court, I would come out of there looking like and feeling like a liar. I was not a liar, but I did not have the strength, the support, or the words to explain what had happened, so I stayed silent. His aggravated burglary charge landed him a sentence of two years. He served one. Even the knife was not considered a premeditated weapon because he always had one with him, I had even told the police this bit of information myself.

Because Jake had been staying with my sister at the time, I had to tell her what had happened because there was no hiding my face and I needed her to prepare Jake for seeing me. I told her about this one incident, but what has struck me in writing this book, was that I have never given much consideration to what went before. What happened up until this point was also traumatic, yet when I have told people about how or why Rowan has nothing to do with her father, all I have to tell them about is this incident, and I don't even have to tell them much about it, for them to fully accept that this would be enough for me to stop access or for me to perhaps have some psychological issues. It is enough, but I don't think until now I have ever given myself any space or any credit for surviving the stuff that happened before. I will.

CHAPTER NINETEEN

I was attacked in August, and in September I started a degree in social work. What? No therapy, no support, years of abuse and I start a degree in social work. I started a degree in social work because I felt I was so good at supporting my sister who had schizophrenia and had such empathy for people that I imagined I would be great in this role. And do you know what? I really was. I wanted to work with people living with mental illness and having seen a line of what I viewed as useless, unsupportive social workers supposedly supporting my sister, I was sure I would never make those mistakes. I had been visited by a representative from Women's Aid after the incident. She had said to me, perhaps I could help you sign up for a little course or something. What a judgmental prick, I had thought. You assumed that as a battered woman I don't have the capacity to educate myself and you think I need your help to get on a little course. What do you suggest I do, needlepoint or knitting? I vowed then never to prejudge a person in this way and make them feel as stupid and helpless as this woman made me feel, and I would like to hope I never have. It has certainly been something that has never left the forefront of my mind, especially in my professional career. I came across this woman when I was indeed a social worker, not I might add working in mental health, but in the field of child protection. She didn't recognise me, but I recognised her.

By the time I had finished my degree T had been in and then out again, of prison. When he came out, he contacted me, but I reported him and while he arrived at my house full of anger about what I had done, he never came back again. I don't know if he went back to prison, or if he is alive or dead to this day.

When I started university, I was still living in that same house but my sisters, who I am eternally grateful for, decided to help me out and they got together and paid a deposit and the mortgage on my house. Angels working their magic again. The obvious route now was that I would finish uni, be qualified as a social worker, get a well-paid job, and pay the mortgage myself and pay them back. To get to Jake's school you had to walk down this long road of red brick terraced houses. They were just like the ones I had imagined in *Milly Molly Mandy* and each day that I walked up and down this street I would look at all the different gardens and the different ways each person had given these identical houses their individual identity. I used to go mad at my mother for doing this, for looking in people's gardens. They can't see me, she would say, they don't mind, I'm just looking at their flowers and admiring their work. I often think about that when look into people's gardens as I walk past now. I saw a house for sale in this street and I put in an offer. The sale took forever, and I moved in on the 19th of December. This time, I was organised; gifts bought and wrapped for the children and my ex sister in law had us for Christmas dinner that year. Bit weird having Christmas dinner with my ex-husband who was also there visiting, as he usually did, but it was all right. We were always able to get along, he is, like most people, generally a good man. He has his own childhood tales to tell which have shaped him as an adult but those are his not mine to tell. I had a boyfriend at the time. It strikes me that in my life I have never spent much time alone, even though I had been technically single for years by that point, T's presence had meant that I was never physically alone for very long. My boyfriend had two children around Rowan's age, he seemed to really like me, he had a good job, but in truth he was pretty boring to me. He had a very domineering mother who looked down her nose at me, or so I felt, because here I was, single mother, two kids to two different men, likes to wear makeup, probably a slut, and unless you start to explain to everyone the whole sordid tale, this is inevitably the conclusion they come to, in my experience. I wanted his attention, even though I didn't actually enjoy spending time with him. It made no sense until I did this work upon myself and made a few discoveries about my brain that made all of this clear, or clearer, but I will move onto that later. This sort of rubbish half-hearted relationship where I barely even saw this man, lasted until one night when I was out, drunk, and I slept with a stranger, who was extremely good looking and who gave me a great deal of attention, which I loved, and invited me back to his house. It was a mix between a finger up at my boyfriend for being such an absent partner and an almost craving for some excitement, but it was mainly because I had once again done something rash, without thinking, and was not really sure how to control the situation. It certainly was not because all I cared about was having some sex and anyone would do. At this point, sex was something I did for others not for myself.

My own stupid luck, a few weeks later I discovered I was pregnant. My boyfriend couldn't have children, so I knew unequivocally it wasn't his. I had an abortion, another one. Shame, shame, shame, Guilt, guilt, guilt.

This relationship ended, no surprise there. I felt unaffected by it. And just like that, seemingly out of my control another man came into my life. He was a relative of someone a friend of mine knew, so in a way this led me to think he was safe. He was a lot older than me, and he seemed alright, I kind of liked him. He asked me out on a few dates. This was me trying to be good. We met and took the kids to the fair; he had a daughter the same age as Jake, and this seemed positive for us all. He began to stay at my house and then his belongings started to stay at my house and then he stayed less at his house and all the while I started to feel like I wasn't as keen on him as I first thought.

I was in my final year at uni. He had wormed his way into my life on several false pretences. He was ex-navy, and now worked on the oil rigs, allegedly, but he had been off work for a while now because of a shoulder injury. He had a number of business plans, even one that I helped him set up, but he had no money and I thought I was rolling in it after being on benefits and now being eligible for student loads and all sorts of uni grants, so I began to pay for everything and give him money, just while he got himself back on his feet.

Alongside this my father was beginning to get ill. He was deeply depressed. He started talking about the past, about my mother and how sad he was about her death. I don't know if this started it, but this was what I knew. After his cruel letter I did not speak to him and my Granny Katherine, which I have to say hurt so badly I couldn't bear it at times. I looked up to this woman so much, the thought that she didn't like me in any way broke my heart. When Rowan was born, I just went up there and visited them. I ambushed him in a way, and he couldn't ignore me. We began to talk again but he made it clear what he thought of me at every opportunity.

It is all a traumatised mess in my brain so I can't even now tell you exact conversations or events that would demonstrate what this man, my new boyfriend, did. It was so subtle at first, even now I can't say but I do know this. My brain at the time was in a traumatised state. When I hear the phrase, 'it's ok not to be ok' I want to correct it. No. It is not ok not to be ok, it's really dangerous not to be ok! I know that's not what they mean, but when you are not OK, you are at risk. This man manipulated me into giving him money, he stole from me, and he somehow made me believe that once again he had saved me and he had provided something Rowan at the least, would never have, a father. He would fill this role, he even tried to adopt her at one point, but this was one of the glowing bright as the sun red flags I saw. Somehow, with his abusive magic he made me think that I had to stay with him, marry him, or I would be damaging Rowan, which of course was something I did not want to do in any way shape or form. It's what happened anyway, regrettably. I felt such huge, heavy regret in my body and mind. We got married and I remember the day before the wedding thinking to myself. You can do this, even if it's just until the kids grow up, you can do it and it will all be alright, just keep your head down and be good. After all, I thought, I'd been through worse. I had at the time. My father reluctantly came to the wedding. He made no effort to hide his dislike of this man. At the wedding, my father seemed in good spirits, dancing and drinking, but after that it all changed. This was when he really went downhill mentally, and this is when it got really bad for me too. My husband never went back to work because he said he had developed a condition that meant he wasn't allowed back on the rigs. This may have been true, but I don't think it was. He never contributed to the cleaning business I helped him set up, and it folded because after all I was in my last year at university and had a lot more to do and think about. He began to boss the kids about, Jake especially, and Jake being Jake didn't back down which turned out not to work in his favour. I would not allow him to speak to Jake in that way, so I got it instead, which I never minded of course, but I was scared to have him in the house, and everyone walked on eggshells so as not to upset him. He once stood over me in the kitchen screaming and shouting so loud at me it hurt my ears and he said to me,

"I will shout and shout until I break you down and you will not be able to get back up."

Those were his exact words; I can hear them now. I have never forgotten. The times and dates are all a bit of blur, trauma to the brain makes some things clear and others not. It means victims of crime often have their testimonies disregarded because they appear incoherent.

My father had tried to kill himself perhaps once or twice that year. I had been to visit him but as I went to leave, he begged me to come back. It was surreal to witness my father in this position. This man, who had dominated me in many ways, was now almost childlike, crying and begging me to help him. Even on the phone he would ring me and say to me,

"I'm going to die, this distress, it's going to kill me."

"I need to take the kids home, they are back at school tomorrow," I'd told him, "But I will come back without them and see you, ok?"

It was in the sort of way you appease an upset child. Once the children were settled back at home I turned straight back around. I drove out of the street and drove for around 20 minutes and pulled over. My father needed me, and I wanted more than anything to go and help him, but I could not leave my children with this man, it was not going to happen. My soul was speaking to me. In the weeks that passed I spent a lot of my time simply negotiating my life and the children's lives in ways that meant we spent the least time with this man. I had asked him to leave but he refused. I talked to him, I told him that I no longer cared for him, and he would agree that he would leave and then the next day he would pretend the conversation had never happened. I was really unsure of how to get him to get out. I had often tried to get T to get out, but I could not, and here I was again. A recurring nightmare that I had for years was that either or sometimes both of these men were in my house, and I couldn't get them to leave and that I was trapped. Very scary and very real.

I got a job as a child protection social worker in June 2007. A week before I was due to start, my father went missing. The Saturday before I was due to start my job, I was sitting on the sofa watching *You've Been Framed*. I think Rowan was in bed and Jake was upstairs and a knock came at the door, and he answered it. He had been in the kitchen where the front door was. He put his head through the door and said to me, the police are here. I went through and two police officers were standing in my kitchen, and they asked if they could sit down and if I wanted to sit down. By this time, I was standing next to the washing machine, but a load of wet washing was lying on the floor, and it seemed so small in the room with him and these two figures in their large jackets, that the only place I had to stand was on the wet washing and I can feel the damp on my bare feet now.

"We have found a body who we believe to be your father" was something like the words they said to me.

Whether they told me he had killed himself, whether they did not, I don't know, but that's what had happened. My father had driven to a spot in the woods and gassed himself and some poor woman walking her dog had found him. He went to hold my hand and I recoiled. You, I thought, are nothing to me. You and your revolting words and actions can get off me right now. Everything in that moment changed, how could it not have? A sudden realisation that people do kill themselves. I had thought about it many times, as you might imagine, but I hadn't done it. My kids stopped me, but I wasn't good enough to stop my father. He left me. I postponed my work start date for two weeks. Holy shit girl, did nobody notice or think to themselves that this was not appropriate? Of course they didn't, because I smiled, and I kept it all together because this is what I did, and this was how I put one foot in front of the other each day. Pack it all inside and get on with it.

The police asked me to come and identify my father's body. I was to come as soon as possible, so the next morning he drove me up to the police station in Perth. I was in a real hole here. I didn't want him to come yet I didn't want to leave the kids with him, so to protect them I asked him to come with me and I left the kids with his sister who I didn't really know, and the kids certainly didn't, but I had to hope that she was a safer bet than him. When we arrived at the police station, they sat me in a room and the plan had been for them to drive me from there to the morgue where my father's body was, but as soon as I arrived, they suddenly changed their mind. Frankie, my father's partner, who unluckily for her but not for me, had given up her life in Australia to come and live with my father and now found herself in this shit show, said to me she believed that when they saw me, so young and obviously not actually in a fit state to identify a body that had been decomposing in the hot windscreen of a car for a few days, they had changed their mind. She was probably right. I sat in the room with an officer, and he took what you might call a statement from me. Asking me about my father, how he had been, what had been going on prior to this event. He was so incredibly kind and respectful to me that I never wanted to leave. It was the first bit of kindness and support I had been shown for I can't remember how long.

My husband had made sure he did not leave my side, in fact he never let me leave his side and wanted to know where I was at all times and would check and follow me. So, he sat in on the interview with the officer, but he was not included in any of the conversation, and I just knew this had rubbed him up the wrong way.

"He was a total cunt, wasn't he?" he said when we got outside. "He fancied you, thank God I was here, or he'd probably have had you bent over that table."

That is honestly what he said to me. I heard him but I didn't respond. We went home but no sooner had I returned then I had to go back, I can't remember why but I was his next of kin so there were things I had to do. Richard, my father's best friend, had been appointed as executor of my father's will, thank goodness because I would not have had a clue what to do. Another angel at my side. Once again, my husband drove me in the van and the children stayed with his sister. I did not plan to be away long. We were at my father's house and at this point I had not cried. I had not been able to show any emotion about what had happened at all, I just couldn't do it. I felt like Richard, his wife, Frankie and him were all looking at me for a reaction and I couldn't let them see any cracks. You can't see my pain; I am going to bed. To bed in this weird space that is my beloved childhood home, that I was forced to leave but here I am back, and it is not how I remember it. None of the people I used to love are here. My bedroom walls are here but it isn't my room. I lay in the bed regardless and tried to soak in any tiny amount of comfort that might have been remaining from the past.

I had a number of official things to do in Perth the next day, the death certificate had been released so we drove there on the way back home and my body continued on. I had no idea really what I was doing, and it was bit like a board game. Each place that I went to gave me new instructions on where to go next. My husband had been brewing the whole time we had been away. He felt like I wasn't interacting with him as I should be, and I wasn't reacting to my father's death in the way that I should do. I lost it. I screamed at him that I had told him now repeatedly that I wanted nothing more to do with him. My father's death had not changed this, and I wanted him out. I got out of the van, and I said to him that I would get the train home that I could no longer sit another moment in his presence.

Often, especially as women, we are told that anger is an undesirable emotion, but without anger where is the motivation? The energy of anger can fuel change, it can accelerate it, and I was feeling angry. Off I marched and collected my father's death certificate, and they told me I then needed to take this to the funeral directors, they pointed one out to me from the window and I went to the next destination. I wasn't even sure what I needed to say to said director. I had no appointment, but a smart looking man with an old kind face, let me in and in a while, we had come together with a plan for my father's funeral. He had it written on a piece of paper on his desk. Then who would have thought it, prick face barges in (you know who I mean), the way he always did, full of resentment, and sat down next to me. I froze and I am quite sure the funeral director saw me. He leant over onto the funeral director's desk and whipped up the list he had been making.

"What's this you have been writing?" he said, "What have you been talking about?"

I was frozen in time, my body and mind a mix of fear and mortification.

"You're going to have to hurry up, I'm parked on double yellow!" he shouted at me.

Then the funeral director stood up and he invited him to stand too, then he walked him calmly to the door. He opened the door and pointed down the street, he said to him,

"Right at the bottom there is a place you can park, it's free and no double yellow lines. You go and park down there and Silvia will be with you when we have finished."

As if under a magic spell, Twat Head (you still know who I mean) followed his instructions and left. The funeral director returned and sat down and carried on with our conversation as if nothing had happened. It was not in a way that he was embarrassed or wasn't sure what to say or he wished not to embarrass me further. It was in a way that said to me, that angry man is of no importance to us, we shall not give him any more of our attention or energy. Another angel.

I came out of the funeral directors and walked down to the van where Idiot Man sat. Feeling brave and energised by the strength of the funeral director, I reminded him of my decision to take the train home and said he would be wasting his time waiting any longer for me. I walked off. He screamed after me and I became a little less brave. He told me I had to first go with him to the petrol station to fill up the van as he had no money, and I was not about to give him my bank card, so I reluctantly agreed. He filled up the van and he started to drive off on the promise that he would take me to the train station but then he started to drive fast, and I suddenly felt scared.

"Let me out!" I screamed.

He stopped the van, and I opened the door but as I stepped out, he drove off again leaving me hanging out the door. I pulled myself in somehow and he proceeded to drive back and forth across the street, crisscrossing this way and that, into oncoming traffic, people running out of the way. I'm serious, how nobody was killed or injured, bar myself of course, I do not know and somehow nobody called the police, at least to my knowledge. I believed I was going to die, that he would kill me. He kept on driving, out of the town and back on the road to Newcastle. I was not getting out and I shut my eyes and tried to sleep so I could distract myself until I got back home to my children. I made a firm promise to myself to get him out and after much fighting and arguing over the coming weeks he eventually left on the condition that I paid for his deposit on his house and the furniture he needed. It was a small price to pay but it was not the end. My father had left me as sole beneficiary to his estate and Arsehole (you still know who I mean), was after it, being the greedy, lazy thief that he was.

One such example of his lack of even basic morals led me into yet another very difficult and upsetting situation. He fraudulently took out a mobile phone contact in my name using my bank account. He frequently stole money from me, and this must have been right before he left, as I never saw the phone, but he was also extremely stupid, so when the phone bill popped onto my letter box, I could clearly see what he had done but he had managed to build up a bill of over £100 in this first month. I rang the phone company and explained, and they immediately cancelled the contract. His house was over 25 miles from where I lived. The very next day early in the morning as I was getting ready to go to school and work, he walked in the door, furious, shouting at me for cancelling his phone. He told me that he had seen what I had done, and he had had to walk from his house to sort it out because he had no money. I failed to see why his predicament would be any of my concern, but in his plain arrogance he could not even see that he was the one who had just stolen over £100 from me, just to add to the rest, and he had more than a brass neck complaining about me deciding I didn't want to pay for his extortionate phone bills. I had been at the door when he had arrived, so as we argued I was moving closer to the door and when he stepped outside, I saw my chance, shut the door and locked it. He tried to pull at the handle, stopping me from locking it, but he failed, and I was safe.

"You're fucked" he shouted through the letter box, "big mistake!"

I decided to report the incident to the police. If I had learned anything from my past experiences, it was that unless it's recorded it hasn't happened, according to the police. Even then it's a bit dubious as to the attention they will give it, but this somehow felt like a threat, so I rang them, and they said an officer would be round that day to speak to me. An officer arrived within about 10 minutes, which I was surprised about, but then he said that he had just spoken to Knob Head. Wow, great, I thought, these are on the ball today. No. He had just spoken to him because when the enormous cretin left my house, he had gone to the police station and lied to them. He told them I had assaulted him, pushed him out of his house and to the ground and that I had injured his shoulder. The officer said that while he was reporting an assault and I was reporting just a possible threat, it was likely that should this be taken further, I would be the one arrested and not him. I was in total shock. I had an appointment at the police station to be arrested. I had to drive myself willingly to the building, walk in, let them put me in a cell and listen as they arrested me. Then I was booked in to be interviewed. I had to stand there and give them my name and my profession and tell them that I was a social worker, employed by the local council in the role of protecting children, and here I was being arrested for assault. He knew the consequences of his lie for me and my life, this is why he did it. Nothing about his story measured up, and while I wasn't lying about what had happened, the charge was dropped. I had to tell my employer and mortified doesn't even begin to cover how I felt.

Months of solicitor's letters passed between us as I tried to divorce this hideous character. He put in a counter claim for divorce, claiming I had cheated on him and claims for as much money as he could get his hands on. The letters and fantastical claims that he made became almost funny. In the end he was awarded £14,000 and I had to agree to his divorce claim and say that I had cheated on him, because he denied having ever received my petition, and honestly it made zero difference to me. My divorce solicitor rang me when it was all over, and she said to me,

"Well, Silvia, what are we to do for our amusement now?"

CHAPTER TWENTY

I had been at my new job as a social worker for a few months when I began to feel quite unwell, mentally. To manage the life situations, and by manage, I mean block out, I had periodically been prescribed antidepressants by my GP. I had taken them for a while, but they never worked to change how I felt. The amount of trauma I had in my brain needed letting out, not to be masked with some tablets, so they never even touched the sides. I pushed myself through because I had to, but it was extremely tiring. I had never even considered it, but a woman at work suggested I take some time off. Great plan, I thought, is it as easy as that, you just get to take time off work and still get paid? I was finding my job role very overwhelming for a number of reasons. The cases I dealt with were extremely close to my own experiences. I had to admit that my children, who had been present for some of the abuse; Rowan who had had a knife held to her neck, they were at risk and had suffered harm. I knew that already, but in my role, I had to face it every day and this was rough going. The real conflict came when I was in the presence of professionals who made judgments of parents, mainly mothers I might add, who were being abused. 'Failure to protect.' This was a phrase often used in assessments and court papers. A mother failed to stop a violent man entering her home, putting her children at risk of emotional and physical harm, therefore she failed to protect. It was a bit like when my father had written that letter to me saying all the things I had imagined he thought of me, confirming my possible paranoia to be true. Women in abusive relationships, single mothers with children to different men, were judged as lower-class citizens, as provocateurs, as reckless, as unfit to look after themselves or their children. Here I was on the other side of the fence looking over at these women in a place of judgment and authority. My soul was not comfortable here. In my role as a social worker, I was again an outsider because I could not and would not be like the others, who judged from a place of little or no experience. There were a few coworkers along the way who I felt a slight connection to, but on the whole these people were not my tribe. I came to work, did my job, and left. I wasn't rude, I didn't actively distance myself, but perhaps subconsciously I did. I showed my face at nights out and events, I did my duty, but I did not belong. I went into social work to work for the clients. You would think that would be most people's motivation but, let me tell you, it is not. They may pretend, even to themselves, that they are the moral compass, the instructor of good, the ones who will protect and see justice served, but most simply want to control, and this is what drives them. It's not lightly that I say that. It's hugely sad that people's lives are literally in the hands of individuals who have not got an effing clue what they are going through, nor do they care or have the time to find out. I made time. I am not saying that in my role children were not taken into care, adopted even, because it did happen, but I can 100% guarantee that this was when every other possible avenue had been explored. I did this at the risk of criticism from management and colleagues and at the risk of dismissal. A client once said something in a meeting about me and it was one of my proudest moments as a social worker, and also as a person. This woman who was only in her early 20s at the time, had been in care herself, she had been in prison, in violent relationships, had absent parents, and her first child had been taken from her at birth. This is such a common story that I am not identifying her by stating these facts. All the reports about her from childhood to when I met her said that she was obstructive and unable to work with professionals. At this meeting, the chairperson said to her,

"In the past few months, you have engaged really well, all these reports are very positive, and you seem to have really opened up to the social worker." This was me. "What's changed?" the chair asked her, and she turned to her and said quite simply,

> "Silvia listens to me, and nobody has ever done that before."

There it is again. Gratitude. Not that I wanted the gratitude from her, it was the gratitude I felt towards her. Floods and floods of it rushing through my soul, and it was in truth this girl that kept me in my role. I knew that when I left it would all turn to shit for her, and it did.

Was my approach affected by my own experiences? Absolutely yes. Was I fully aware of that at all times? No. Did this ever put children at risk? No, although you can never be 100 percent sure of how your actions affect others, especially children. Did this role trigger and aggravate my trauma on a daily basis? Yes.

CHAPTER TWENTY- ONE

A friend of mine and her husband set me up on a blind date with one of his mates from work, Brian. Sure thing I said, I will go along to that. I promise this isn't another couple grooming me for sex with their friends story. This was good, this was nice, safe, and 'normal'. Two people being introduced to each other through mutual friends who liked and cared about them. For me, a chance to be good.

I had shared with husband 2, what had happened to me with T and how he ended up in prison. The narcissist often used this against me. He could see why someone would treat me like that, he would say. No wonder he hit you the way you are. One thing I wish I hadn't done is share any of this with Brian I felt I had to because it felt like part of me and I wasn't oblivious to the fact that it had changed me, but the truth is, that never affected him, he made no allowances for the trauma and how this may manifest itself, ever, and when we separated, he used it against me too. Somehow this was worse because I suppose I expected more. Perhaps he was the first person I had actually loved, perhaps I thought he loved me, so therefore it was worse to hear it from him.

Brian was as reliable and as level-headed as a person could be. He was organised whereas I was very disorganised. He was tidy whereas I was messy. He knew and remembered all the facts about important things and events and appointments, whereas I didn't. He didn't hit me, or shout at me directly, he didn't expect me to dress a certain way, or be a certain way, to look after him in any way, and for a very long time this ying to my yang was exactly what I needed. Exactly the kind of grounding force my chaotic brain needed. He was fun too, he would organise nice things for us to do together and we were interested in a few of the same things, such as travel and walking, eating out, having a drink. He loved football and took Jake to the match, he was a stable person for Rowan, although he did find her much harder to bond with. They had very little in common but, you know, it was acceptable. I think that if I had been more stable in my mind we might have stayed together longer, and when I say that I am not putting all the responsibility for our breakup on myself, but Brian did not like upset and change and I was a whole heap of upset and so accustomed to change, my self-sabotaging brain would make change happen even if it was in my very worst interests. I had been married twice before. Both times I didn't have much money and they were sad affairs, mainly because of the sad circumstances, but nonetheless the pathetic plate of corned beef sandwiches at the reception amplified this. When Brian and I married, we had enough money, together, not one sided, to hold a wedding with table decorations, and a meal. Coordinated seat coverings and flower arrangements. My inner child, the lover of and believer in fairy tales, she was in her element. We had planned the wedding, sent out save the date cards, spent an afternoon with my friends trying on wedding dresses that I could actually afford, and it was as close to normal as I dared to enjoy. Was this it, had I finally made it at being good?

I certainly aimed to embrace this illusion as much as I could that's for sure. So why not decided to have a child together as well? I could get it right and everyone would be happy for me and say kind things like, 'Congratulations on your happy news' or 'How are you feeling, how is your pregnancy going? Let me know if you need anything.'

Having had only 'unplanned' pregnancies it was a shock to me that this took a long time to happen. I got more and more obsessed and fixated upon getting pregnant and also wondering what was wrong. My hatred and disgust for myself at having two abortions meant I concluded that this was my fault. I remembered what the consultant had said to me.

"You do know that this procedure will mean you might not be able to have children again, is that what you want?"

Is it, is it stupid girl? I am sorry, no it isn't, I want this baby, I am sorry! Shame, Shame, Shame. We eventually fell pregnant, but I knew immediately something was not right. I was not ill, not even a slight feeling of nausea. I just knew. Mothers' instinct, my soul, it told me and at about 10 weeks into the pregnancy we lost the baby. At the hospital Brian said to me, "Well, I can't go through this again, guess we aren't going to have a baby."

I felt such fury towards him at that moment and my real instincts kicked in. How dare you even suggest such a thing, how dare you! And I think that was it. The day the seed was planted in my brain that perhaps this man was not as safe and as perfect as I had decided he was. I know this makes no sense now, but it made sense to me. Nobody is perfect, and what he said was not a bad thing to say. He was upset too; he might have well thought that he didn't want to risk the upset again. Totally valid emotions and thoughts to have. My brain was not able to compute this.

Animal-like instinct is all I can describe it as. The urge to reproduce was like nothing I have felt before or since. Within a month I was pregnant again. Rowan was nine or ten throughout my pregnancy and Jake much older, and while he was still living at home, he was preoccupied with his own life, girlfriend, college and all the things he should have been preoccupied with. I had suffered with hyperemesis when I was pregnant with Rowan but with this baby it was on another level. Months of constant sickness left my body in quite a state. I was admitted to hospital on a few occasions which was actual bliss. They pumped me full of fluids via a drip and it was better than any spa experience, I can tell you. The relief was immense, but as soon as you perked up a bit, they sent you home and it started again. I cried one day; I just couldn't take it and even considered an abortion just to make it all stop. Poor Rowan helped me and had to fend for herself a lot of the time. I didn't have the capacity to play with her or do anything with her for a few months at least. Brian did the basics. Fed her, washed her clothes, took her to school if he wasn't at work, but the thing was, he was so very often at work and when he wasn't at work, he was never prepared to change his plans of going to the pub with his friends, even when his partner was unwell in bed. Another seed of doubt planted. Could I count on this man after all? I thought I could but perhaps I had made a big mistake. Again. After the sickness subsided, I got this other condition where my hips sort of gave way. It was painful to the point where I needed crutches to walk. I was off work for almost all of my pregnancy which was the only good thing to come out of it.

By the end of my pregnancy, I was an absolute physical wreck. Jasmine was born on 18th June 2012, 15 days overdue and after an induced labour. The labour planted more seeds of doubt in my mind. While draped over the back of the bed, I dropped the gas and air tube.

"Quick get it!" I shouted to Brian.

"Calm down," he snapped at me, as he begrudgingly put down his phone and passed me the mask.

I didn't say anything, but it was logged. My brain, remember, was on high alert for anything that put me or the kids at risk. The phone was already a bone of contention between us. He was addicted to looking at his phone and the more he looked at his phone the less he was present in the world or with us, his family. When Florence was born, the first thing he did was pick up his phone and ring his mother, not come over to me or hold Florence. I said to him. Please just wait, just give us these first moments just for us. He couldn't, I could see it, he just couldn't do it, so I sat in the bed, and I watched him as he rang this one and that one thinking to myself, where are you?

Six weeks later we got married. My soul was alerting me to the seeds, but I did not listen, I ignored myself yet again and clambered on regardless. It was a running joke that Brian couldn't walk slowly because of his job as a postman. He could never switch off and stroll along, so when we had finished our vows, we ran back down the aisle and we were greeted in the corridor with a glass of champagne. Just the two of us, and it was the only moment that day where he actually looked at me and we were together. I look back on that moment with true happiness still to this day. It felt like a long time, but it probably wasn't, and suddenly everyone had caught up and followed us, and there it was, we were in the throes of the celebration. He didn't take care to look after the baby that day, I did, and my sisters did. He didn't get up with her at 4am and feed her, I did that, and so sadly and regrettably this is how it went from then on. I did it all, despite specifically telling him that I didn't want to do it all myself again. I was so frustrated with myself for getting myself and the children into another situation that just wasn't right. Still not right! I had a well-paid job, a nice husband, a big house, a fucking hot tub even and it was still not right. I was not OK, and this was not OK.

After my pregnancy and Florence's birth I experienced postnatal depression absolutely compounded by the lack of sleep I had with this child, and the utter disappointment that I had screwed it up again. These were the very last straws my mind and my body could take. My soul? Well, she was barely even there.

CHAPTER TWENTY-TWO

My therapy journey, as I have alluded to already, started with a counsellor. I was awarded six sessions and it was in this time that she told me I had what is called Chronic Post Traumatic Stress Disorder. From what I had discussed with the counsellor, she felt this was caused at the time I was attacked by T. More likely it was before then, but I will never know for sure, and it doesn't matter. She referred me to a domestic violence charity for some specialised support, and I went to that office for 20 weeks straight. Each time I went it stirred it all up again, I regurgitated and relived it all and my body was full of actual pain, week in, week out. The clock would count down until my time was up, and the anxious energy running through my body was almost too much to bear at times. I would curl up in a ball and squeeze myself tight in a bid to make it stop. It was a physical reaction and I often thought I might die from it or at least wondered if I could die so it would stop. Believe it or not, in those 20 hours of talking I didn't share with the counsellor half of what happened. My throat would tighten, I just couldn't physically say what had happened. It was wrapped in so much distress and guilt there were no words. I had started something, but I wanted it to stop because it was all too much, and what I needed was to be cared for with as much care and support a person could be afforded when going through this experience. To be nurtured, made a cup of tea, supported with the care of the children. I needed to rest and to sleep and be fed foods that would nourish me and help me recover. I know now that these were the things I needed. Not big things, not a week in Mauritius, not anything unacceptable to request or indeed need, but they didn't happen and the more I expressed my distress to Brian, the more he backed away. It was as if he could not be around me, like my emotions and my behaviour made his skin crawl. That's how I felt. To tell him how I felt made me disgusted with myself. This tough woman whining on about her emotions, so pathetic, so weak. I had always been able to get up and get on and look at me now, this quivering wreck. For me, expressing how I felt was huge, but it was met with nothing. No support, no reaction even, which is somewhat worse. All he could say was that he just could not relate to how I felt because he had never felt that way. I was not expecting him to understand everything, that is not what I needed. Not safe, my mind was telling me. You need help and this is not a safe space. There is no help here for you, you need to run away. If I could put a time frame on this, I'd say that I felt like this for around two years. Two years of feeling unsafe and trapped and feeling unable to move. So tired, yet so restless. Afraid at all times but confused and annoyed at myself because this was nothing compared to what I had lived through already. Should I feel grateful for this? Should I accept this as a good situation and be satisfied with this as my life, as my husband, because it wasn't as bad as it had been?

CHAPTER TWENTY-THREE

My job was becoming increasingly hard to keep on top of. I couldn't coordinate all the forms and the meetings and also manage to remember milk at the shop for my own kids' cereal. Triggering trauma in my counselling sessions, triggering trauma at work, at home scared that I was suddenly living with a man who was not the support I thought he was. When the chips were down, he was not present. I wasn't down, not yet and in writing this book it confirms for me that I have, and always have had, the capacity to change things. Even if it's been the smallest bit of positive energy, I have been able to find it and take action to get myself out. Survival. Even at this time when most days I honestly just wanted to die – and I'm not being melodramatic here, I really felt like it would be the ultimate rest and I was so, so tired – even then, my brain was making plans that could help. Solutions. I love a solution to a problem. 'Leave your job' was the idea, and as soon as it popped into my mind, I felt relieved. This was a great idea! You know what, it was a great idea, but it was also a difficult concept to get my head around because securing my professional job proved to everyone who had judged me as the useless stupid single mother, that I was as good as them. I was just like everyone else in my family. I had a degree now and a house and a car and a pension and I didn't have to pretend any of this existed because it did, but one day I suddenly knew in my body that I no longer cared. I always thought I did but I actually couldn't care less. This job was damaging me and all the money in the world did not compensate for it. It was a form of self-harm, and I didn't want to do it to myself anymore. I felt unbelievable guilt at leaving my social work families. They were the ones I cared about, and there are some families, children and parents, that have left an indentation on me, and that I will never forget for a multitude of reasons. But this is the thing, I had made the decision, had the idea and I was going to roll with it, because that is what I do, and I like that about me. Some call it reckless, I call it industrious. I made a further plan to retrain as a counsellor, the course was three years long and at the end I would be a qualified counsellor, hypnotherapist, and psychotherapist. Working with people was what I loved and what I was good at. One thing I never doubted about myself. I was good at working with people. I am good at working with people and supporting them to make changes. With that in mind, I imagined that counselling might be a good fit, but I always remember I wasn't entirely convinced even then.

Hypnotherapy and counselling combined was the first year, then on to specialised counselling the next and finally psychotherapy. It said in the prospectus that if you had relevant qualifications, you could skip the first year. I was sure my social work degree was relevant, but the computer said no. I didn't want to wait any longer than I had to, to finish my study and leave my job, because this was the plan. I would either get a job or start my own practice.

I am forever grateful for that 'no' from the computer because studying the phenomenal art of hypnotherapy was exactly where I was meant to be, and here lies a theory that I have always believed. Even when something seems like it isn't working out, there will be a day that you realise it happened for a reason. I will discuss this further later in this book, but, yes, despite what had gone on so far, I always brought myself back to this belief and this is one such occasion when I was proved correct. I very quickly noticed how much hypnotherapy was helping me in ways that I had never even imagined, that's one for fellow hypnotherapists there, and I made a further decision at this discovery that counselling was no longer in the plan and world-renowned expert hypnotherapist was the actual goal. This stuff had real legs and real power, which is so much more profound and effective than the talking therapies. In my own experience talking had served a purpose, it had brought me to this stage, but that was its limit and anything past, 'getting it off your chest' is just stirring up the painful energy, week by week, hour by relentless hour and I didn't want to spend my days doing that. Talk about synchronicity, as I was coming to the end of my hypnotherapy training there was to be a complete overhaul yet again of children's services. Was this angelic intervention? I worked three days a week at the time, Florence was in nursery, and it was the absolute most I could afford to leave her. Everyone is to reapply for their jobs, we were told, and there will be no more part-time roles.

"What about people who work part-time now?" I asked, already knowing the answer.

'There will be no more part-time roles' was the only explanation. They were offering anyone who did not wish to reapply for their job the chance to apply for redundancy by the end of June of that year. I went for it, of course I did, this was a definite sign to get out now, and while the redundancy payment was only about £4,000 if I remember rightly, it was enough to see me through for a while, and I could manage. I was set to have my last day at work on 30th

June, my 40th birthday as it happened! We were on holiday in May, sitting in a bar drinking a cocktail, when the email came through to my phone. No explanation, just that the offer of redundancy payouts was no longer available.

"I don't care," I said, "I'm still leaving."

Brian being Brian, sensible planner of everything, thought I was being ridiculous.

"I don't care," I said "I can't take it anymore, I don't care about the money. I had it in my mind that I was leaving in one month's time and I'm not going back on it."

As I so often do, I had misread the holiday information and I was informed that actually I wasn't able to leave on 30th June, I owed them a further two weeks. I felt sick to my stomach, so I rang HR and I said to her,

"What would happen if I didn't, and I just left on 30th anyway?"

"Strictly speaking we could take legal action but truthfully, we won't. If you do take this action however it would be unlikely for you to get a positive reference from us if you wanted to get another job."

"A risk I'm willing to take," I said.

I did leave on the 30th, I didn't get prosecuted, and I've never yet had the need or the inclination to ask them for a reference. That's when I started my business, Hummingbird Hypnotherapy, the beginning of this incredible journey of ups and downs in the world of self-employment. I didn't know how to set up or run a business. Minor facts like this were of no concern to me. Brian thought I was being reckless, and selfish and he even said to me once,

    "Hypnotherapy destroyed you."

Hypnotherapy saved me, you idiot, but my new direction did not fit into your plans, so you didn't like it. That's the truth but I say that not with blame. He no longer fitted into what I expected either. I thought I had a partner who would support me no matter what, and he thought he had a normal wife who was content to live a normal life. As I said, if I had been ok then me and Brian might have stayed together longer, because to all intents and purposes he was a good solid person. He didn't do any harm to anyone, he was a canny bloke, people liked him, I liked him! I loved him, I really, really did love that man, and when I discovered that he could not manage me changing, or be with me on this new chapter, I was truly heartbroken. I was a person who had been through a lot of shit and as I healed, I changed. I wasn't the same, I couldn't be. There was nothing I could do about that. If I didn't change, I stayed where I was and that was not an option. In true Silvia style, and that I am sure must have felt out of the blue for Brian I just stopped one day and decided, this is no longer safe, this has to end. I had spent years now attempting to tell this man that I needed his help, that I needed something different from him because I had started something that was changing me, that was scaring me, that was tiring me out. Sadly, I had to conclude in my mind that he was not going to do it. This was a lesson to me. I didn't fully take on board the lesson until my next relationship, and for a good while I felt aggrieved that he wouldn't change for me, be flexible in some tiny way to allow me to fit in. The truth is you cannot expect people to change for you. You might want them to, and they might do it if it works for them, which is great, but you cannot put that expectation onto another person, you just can't. I expected that when I told him I was unwell he would change his routine and his behaviour to support me, but he did not and this to me felt like abandonment. One day I said to him, 'I am so ill, I honestly think I need to go to hospital, to admit myself to a mental hospital'. His response was that I couldn't do that because there would be no one to take the kids to school. This is the level of care and understanding I was faced with, so I came home one day and told him,

"I can't take anymore; we have to separate. Living here with you, so absent from my life, so absent from Florence's life, just consumed with yourself and your phone, I just cannot do it any longer, its simply too hurtful."

CHAPTER TWENTY-FOUR

Brian's reaction to my decision was shock, that's the best way to describe it. Never expect people to act in the way, well, you expect, this will often lead to confusion and upset and a huge dollop of disappointment. You can know it but to learn it and to feel it and accept it, that is different. He was unimaginably angry with me for upsetting his applecart. As you will have gathered, he does not do well with change, the life he had planned with his wife, his kids, his house, his car, and his drinks on a weekend with his friends, was over, this was not what he wanted, and I was the one to blame. All his upset, anger and frustration came my way. All that energy directed right into my soul. Abusive message after abusive message, to the point when once again I was doubting myself. I was a bad person for doing this to him. I was a bad person for doing this to my children again. I was selfish, I was cruel.

That Christmas I went to church to sing carols as I always love to do. I go to the same church my mother attended, it's a small connection to her at Christmas time and I have attempted to go each year since her death and mostly I have managed it. I am not a Christian. I have faith which is not the same as being a Christian, but I was at church, and I thought to myself, well here I am, I might as well give this a go and I prayed right there up to God in his holy house for forgiveness for the terrible crime I had committed. Please, please, please forgive me, I thought, please make him stop. He did not stop, and just today I received a delightful email from him calling me a cunt.

His family didn't forgive me either. In one fell swoop, I lost all my nephews and nieces, with whom I'd had relationships since their births, because now, well, now I was the devil and as punishment for upsetting Brian I was disowned and no longer part of their lives. They wrote abuse about me online, talked disgustingly about me to my child to the point that it was abusive for her. I never had concrete proof of this, but based on what I knew of them, which I will tell you about, this was definitely happening, and they would make no allowances for Florence or any of the other children being in earshot. The way Florence reacted to me, the things she said, they all confirmed my fears, but if I tried to raise the subject, to protest, I was met with further criticism and accused of purposefully causing drama. Gas lit. Nothing could be further from my intention and in time I have learned to feel at peace with myself over this and to be more confident that I am a good mother to that child. They may get something from their tactics, but she will see the truth. Four years on from this as I write, she does. She sees them for who they are, and we work together, her and I, to make sure her little mind is protected from them. It's a work in progress.

CHAPTER TWENTY-FIVE

I saw a quote once 'There is no time limit on your recovery, but you have to start' unknown. I am not writing this book to tell you at the end that I am recovered but I have started. I have started and I am in a good place, so keep reading, it does cheer up a bit in the end, I promise!

So here I was, running my business, a single parent again, selling my house, and dealing with all of the legal rubbish that comes from a separation. Then in true Silvia style, I started a new relationship with Paul. Another hate campaign began to run against me, another helping of guilt and self-doubt in my mind, just to top up the rest, and still in the middle of 'recovery' from PTSD.

I go back a little here to about 6 months before Brian and I separated. I had finished the twenty counselling sessions feeling dreadful. In my hypnotherapy training I had received some relief, but then I happened upon a further course recommended by one of my newfound therapy colleagues. The course was about a technique called Kinetic Shift. In essence, it takes on the concept that emotion is energy, and using this skill of hypnosis and the will of the client it can be 'shifted'. I used to be worried about using the word energy when I talked about therapy as I felt it conjured up an image of someone who faffs about with an incense stick that nobody would take seriously as a therapist or a healer. Firstly, it is not anyone's responsibility to know what may or may not be getting conjured up in a person's mind and secondly, energy is real. We have it, we feel it and we can move it around and it's an actual thing, so if people want to poo-poo that, they are missing out on knowing some pretty essential information about themselves and how to live a great life. It is extremely powerful. This training, which took place in the conference room of a swanky hotel, radically changed the way I worked but was also a time of revelation and reflection for me. Remember, I had created this narrative that I didn't like people, and so far in my life I had stuck with that. In doing this training I realised that I had sat with that story for such a long time that I was in real discomfort when it came to making new connections. This is not a fantastic place to be when your soul is trying to recover. I realised that I had not pursued any new friendships for, well I just couldn't think. I had Emma, and perhaps Josie, because we spent time together as couple friends with Brian and her husband. I had spent physical time with people from work, but even the ones I liked I had not secured friendships with. I had watched the people I knew connect together, seen their photos of girls' nights out on Facebook, of holidays they had taken with each other's families, but I had never felt able to do that. Having no childcare didn't help, but when you say no so many times even though you genuinely can't, people stop asking. This had happened a lot in my life. Then there is the fact that pretending you are ok takes a lot of energy. If you don't see people or have friends who expect you to call them or meet them for coffee, then this isn't an issue. The big one though; if I didn't invest my energy in people, then I couldn't be let down and abandoned by them, and the hurt and rejection would be avoided. I did not have the space for any more of that. Even my friendship with Emma to a certain degree has made me feel rejection at times.

Before I started the Kinetic Shift course, the course leader kept sending me friend requests on Facebook. I was confused, I didn't know her so why would she do that? She emailed me eventually and said that she was trying to add me to a group where everyone could meet each other and offer support, and that also they were all meeting for a meal that night and she wanted to invite me. Not a hope in hell, I had thought. Absolutely no point in having a meal with people I will never see again. It never in a million years occurred to me that this might be a place to meet friends, it was just not a thought in my head anymore. I could have gone, babysitting was not an issue; Brian would be in for the children, but honestly just the thought of it was so unappealing I was almost offended at the request.

The course leader tuned out to be an extremely knowledgeable woman who had worked for many years using more traditional hypnotherapy techniques before discovering this way of using the energy in a person's body to effect change, and by adding in the use of hypnosis we would learn how to bypass the critical mind and empower our clients to trust that negative energy could be found and released at a phenomenal rate. We learned how to invite clients into hypnosis quickly and more effectively than the majority of us had been trained to do so far and to me it seemed to make more sense than anything I had learned so far, as I sat there, so full of the stuff.

Looking round that room at people letting go of emotions in a way that blew our minds, it made mine go in further, but I also observed something else. People in this room had trauma like me. I don't know where it was all from, I didn't need to know, but it was the first time I had been in a room full of people who had a little bit of an understanding, and I do firmly believe I was directed here for this evolution. Added to this, they were also a bunch of people who were open to other and new ways of being, of thinking, of healing. I can now recognise this as the start of me being more open to the idea that there were other people in the world like me. People who were open to new ideas, who didn't think mental health was something to be ashamed of, who were living normal lives but also carrying trauma, and more significantly than that, they were willing to talk about it. Reluctantly, I joined the Facebook group and connected with that group of people, albeit mostly online, and it felt a little bit ok. A tiny bit safe. When my body was convulsing at times due to the pure amount of emotion within it, I contacted one of the people from this course for help. I had not been comfortable letting anything go in front of a whole room during the training itself, that was far too exposing, but I might be able to do it with just one. Andy was his name. Without revealing too much of his life, it's fair to say he had suffered trauma too. We talked, I liked him, I trusted him, and this was quite huge. It was significant for me, and the therapy he offered me helped, it helped hugely. This was so important to me, but Brian and then later even Paul, ruined this somewhat when they accused me of having feelings for this man, and he for me, trying to turn this into something sordid. I saw this as more of a reflection of what they thought of me than what they thought of him but how awful for them to try and tell me that my therapist and friend was only helping me because he wanted to help himself to something else. Disgusting, dirty woman, that's what men see in you. You can be used and sexualised for their pleasure, he wouldn't help you or offer you kindness for any other reason, don't you see? What I do see is that Andy, he helped me regain some power over myself and that to them was a threat. I will be forever grateful that this angel was placed in my path.

"You experienced the pain once and that was enough, you don't have to experience it over and over again anymore"

I say this to my clients but these words, these suggestions from others have the potential to trigger it all again in the blink of an eye. This is why 'recovery' takes time. To be at a place where nothing sparks up those emotions in a way that plumets you to the ground. That's great progress.

CHAPTER TWENTY-SIX

In my move to heal myself I began to learn more and more about energy and in that I was so much more aware of the energy around me, from people and from places and situations. Another major player in the separation between myself and Brian was his family. I will not waste my time or energy writing more than I have to about them, but I will use them as an example of both how I have made positive steps to protect myself and how I have become very aware of the walls I have built around myself. Those walls are not always a support. The walls stopped me finding any enjoyment in life for a very long time, I closed myself off to it all. These people did not have good energy for me. They were in a space where gossiping and finding fault with everyone and everything was normal and constant. I was, and still am, deeply concerned for the impact this would have upon my children. Rowan would cry if she stayed at their house as the kids would punch and fight with each other and their mother would shout and call them names. Brian's mother, I liked her, but she was complacent. She saw it all, but she never said anything. This is how I know for almost certain how badly they will have been talking about me and how much because I had witnessed it for 10 years with my own being. From the way they did it about everyone else, I was certain it would be happening about me.

A pivotal point was after the holiday to Crete. Brian's brother and his wife wanted to renew their vows after she had recovered from throat cancer. She wanted something along the lines of the scene in the film Mamma Mia and it happened that at the time I knew a woman who was Greek and from Crete. She is a woman, a mother, and she had been through a great deal of trauma dealing with cancer, so I was happy to give my energy to supporting her. My friend helped me organise and book the entire wedding service, meal, vows, you name it, and we found a beautiful holiday place with a pool and restaurant, and all was well. We all got dresses and her aunt made little bridesmaid style dresses for the small children. The holiday was booked for me, Brian, Florence and Rowan, along with a host of other family members. A few weeks before we were set to go, Rowan said she wasn't going. She knew. She knew and she wanted no part of it. They didn't understand and I covered it up as best I could, but Rowan was prepared to give up the chance of a week in the sun with a pool and a beach rather than spend a week with them. That was how much negative energy they emitted to us. I admire her and always will for this brave protection of herself. My soul told me the same, but I didn't listen. We even ended up having to fly on my birthday which wouldn't have been such a kick in the teeth had it not been for the fact that 4 days into the holiday another one of the women had a birthday and instead of logically and kindly organising a joint birthday night, the night was only for her. A cake was organised with her name written on it just to make sure it was understood that this was for her and not for me. I spent the week feeling like I was once again the nanny. I watched the children in the pool because I was so worried they would all drown as the other adults sat, not a care on the world, sipping wine in the bar. They organised shopping trips and didn't invite me, it was relentless really and I felt like I was on some awful school trip where all the mean girls were bullying me. Brian just got drunk, and he didn't help either.

After that trip I slept for about two weeks. When I could I just got into bed and slept. My energy was drained and spent. A further trip with the family was planned for later that year. Rowan begged me not to go, she said 'you can't mentally do this', but I didn't know how to get out of it. I did go and I lost my fucking shit on that trip, I wasn't ok.

CHAPTER TWENTY-SEVEN

When Brian and I separated it was distressing and I was in the worst frame of mind psychologically and physically I had ever been in.

"Hey Silvia" my unhinged soul tells me, "Let's start a new relationship with this crazy guy over here! He seems to be going through some serious mental health issues himself, you and your husband have only been separated a few weeks and, honestly, this will add an element of stress your mind will not appreciate, but how's about a bit of a frisk… he seems like a lot of fun!"

And you know, Paul was a lot of fun but of course this was deeply upsetting for Brian and for the children too, and I just thought and hoped it would be alright. Despite a large part of my reason for ending the marriage had been because of Brian's total lack of interest in the children and the upset caused by his absence within the home, it was still a change in what they knew to be safe, and I upset all of that in one go and introduced them to a new adult figure. This is another thing that I added to my list of things titled 'why the fuck did you do that?' This is a really long list by the way, but I do have answers to a fair few of them and the ones I don't, well those answers will be found, even if the answer is there is no answer so now you must move on. John said I have an almost obsession with resolution. I need to know why and what and conclude on almost anything. Unanswered questions do not sit well with me.

Why did I jump straight into the relationship with Paul? I do know that I was in desperate need of someone to hear me and he did. I needed to secure the decision that the relationship with Brian had ended and one way to do this was to be in a new one. That was pretty conclusive. I was craving some fun and some excitement. I like to make my life complicated, and perhaps this is a form of self-harm even, because while it may feel bad it is still a feeling. When you have lived with trauma feelings are quite disjointed and sometimes you feel none at all, so it does give you a kind of painful yet satisfying hit. I was still in a state of mind where I was not in control so I let the situation dictate what happened and most of all I thought Paul was a genuine man who would support me and who would understand me and would support and understand my children. This last one is the real truth, although the others came into play for sure. My brain, as always, was seeking out this perceived safety. Did I fully trust myself to make these decisions? Absolutely not. And in this I was in a strange state once again of taking risk, seeking safety, and feeling deeply unsure. This is a very unsettling and unstable state. This was not an unusual state of mind for me, and I would say that bar a couple of years maximum when I lived with Brian and everything was really calm and normal, I cannot think of a time when this had not been the case, where I had not felt like this is varying intensities. I would even go as far to say that the 'normal' years were even more distressing because I didn't understand them because of the unfamiliarity.

Brian did of course discover I was in a new relationship and his family had a field day with this one. They reached a clear conclusion to what I imagine they could not understand before. It seems they like a resolution too. Before, it seemed like I had ended our marriage for no reason and left Brian without his home and family. In essence I had single-handedly ruined all he knew about his life without justification. When they found out about Paul, they were able to conclude that I must have been having an affair and Paul was the reason I ended the marriage. That made more sense to them, so they went with that despite it being untrue. It being untrue did not stop them writing all about it on social media. It being untrue did not stop them talking so badly about me that five years on the children in the families have a deep hatred for me that they express to my child. I feel the hatred they have for me and for a long time I took it. I had upset this man, and their words and his impacted so deeply upon me. I felt they were justified, and I allowed their hatred to penetrate me and my life. A text message or an email from Brian would hit me so energetically that I would be physically wounded, sometimes for days, and my mind, well, my mind would be simply mashed.

CHAPTER TWENTY-EIGHT

As I write this book, I am increasingly conscious of who might read it. So it is with even more trepidation that I do write this extremely personal book, and am aware, for this chapter in particular, that my children may read these words. I could tell them not to of course, but if they wanted to, they most definitely would.

Hello, dear children.

My little Rowan is a force. This is a short description, but I mean it with all the intention and depth that the word force suggests. To guide, instruct, or mould this child was a near impossible task. I am also a force, but no match for this now woman and certainly no match for that child. As a woman she has learned to tame the fiery side of her force on occasion, so I feel it less, but I feel it.

At the age of sixteen, Rowan had some plans to work in the theatre industry, she had made some contacts and worked on shows backstage from the age of fourteen where she quite deliberately left school whenever she felt like it to do so. I couldn't stop her, but I didn't really want to. I held back the damnation from the school for her so she could carry on. Little Rowan made her way and I looked at that child and thought that no entity in this world would ever knock her down. She supported me too. She cared for me; she nurtured me. This child held me up at times when I couldn't hold myself, and for this I am forever grateful and sorry in equal measure.

When she left school, she began to seem a little lost, and she was really pleased when after walking the streets handing out her CV to shops and cafes in a bid to get a job and save up some money, she landed a job in a small café that sold sushi and katsu curry and dumplings. Great for us as she brought home free food too. She worked long hours, and they gave her a lot of responsibility. She was extremely tired a lot of the time and I advised her to work less but she would not of course. As time went on, she had more and more complaints about the way they treated her. Not paying her as much as the others, fewer bonuses, that sort of thing and while I knew this seemed unfair to her, I assumed this was simply due to her age and the quite frankly unfair restrictions they have about paying people, no matter their age, a fair wage. Nonetheless, I feel like I kept a close eye on things after that, but not a close enough eye as it turned out. Brian had not long moved out and she told me she had been seeing one of the men from the café. He was 24, I think, at the time, and she had just turned seventeen in the August. She opened up to me, which was great, but she shrugged it off, this was no big deal, it wasn't a relationship, they weren't putting labels on it and the like. He didn't want her to tell anyone at work. HUGE ALARM. I said to her in so uncertain terms that the reason he didn't want anyone to know is because this was a complete abuse of power, he should not be dating a 17-year-old girl and he knew it. I don't know if she took this on board at all. I know she has now, but at the time she was excited about the attention from him, I get that. He treated her badly, he manipulated her, shouted at her, humiliated her. I didn't get the entire truth of this until later which is sadly so very often the way. She was unhappy, she wasn't mature enough to deal with this man or see him off. Justice will come to him, as it always does.

Rowan had the idea that moving to Glasgow would open up some more doors for her and the career she wanted, so she decided to move in with my sister. On reflection breaking ties with this man may have been part of the motive for this move, although she didn't say so. The move was not what she had expected either, much to her disappointment, and I was very troubled to see this change in her. In the end, she returned home. To me it seemed impossible that this should even be a problem for her. Whatever she did would be great, whatever she chose she could change if she wanted to. I knew she had all the qualities to be free with her choices, try things, make plans, change plans. What I would have given to have such choice, but I suppose we can find it hard to appreciate what we have always had, and we can also find it even more of a challenge to hear this advice from our parents. She didn't see her options, which I understand. It all seems so permanent and serious at that age.

She came back home, and she was with me when the abuse from Brian and his family tore me down to tears night after night. I didn't want to cry or like to cry so anything that brought me to tears was strong. She was a welcome addition at home for me but for her it was not so. Rowan decided to go back to the café and see if they would give her some work. They did but she only went there for a week and never returned. I knew something was wrong but despite asking her over and over she wouldn't tell me and shut any conversation off about it.

Between then and the next part of the story we moved out of the house, stayed with Jake for a while and then Rowan and Florence stayed with Brian for a while until we found our new home. This was due to a long and complicated house selling and buying process and I will not bore you with the details, but it was yet another unsettling time for everyone.

Then one day as I collected her and Florence from Brian's home to spend the day together, Rowan turned to me and said she was pregnant.

In that one moment a tidal wave – no, wait that's too small – two tidal waves and a tsunami of emotions surged through me. A surge of sadness, grief, anger, confusion, disbelief, even numbness, just engulfed me and I don't even recall the words that fell from my mouth, although I am quite sure she does. In one fell swoop, I saw her life. It was my life. I did not wish her, my beautiful Rowan, to have my life. I did not want her to have to sacrifice and suffer. I wanted her to have as many choices and fun times and experiences as she could and, as I know for a fact, when you have a baby at the age of seventeen about 99% of those choices are down the pan. My children, I do not wish you away. Don't misunderstand me, but what I told Rowan at the time is this, when you have a child, you no longer matter to yourself as much as you did before you had a child. That is how it should be and that is how it is so I knew that once she had her baby in her arms, that baby would take priority. I wanted her to have time to only think about herself. I don't even remember a time when I had that. I had the choice, and I chose to have you children, but as you older ones know, life has been tough. Life may have been easier with more support and family; it may have been. Life may have been easier had a lot of things been different, but when Rowan told me this news and the extra bit of this news that she wanted to continue with the pregnancy and be a mother, I felt the weight of that struggle fall upon me in the entirety of its twenty plus years. It was heavy, and if we are talking about downpours onto my jacket that was beginning to dry out a tad, this downpour flowed like a river during a storm onto me and I sat down under the water in the dark for some time.

When I came out of the depths of that water to care for my girl, as I had to without question, it took all my strength and regrettably there was little left for anything or anyone else. This included Paul, Florence, my business, Jake, and anyone else. I had to come out and move house and care in some way for Florence and care in some way for my business, but I was not me and I was not present. My body might have been seen doing these things, but inside I wasn't. I was under the water. I remember at the time Paul wanted me and needed me and I needed him too, but I had not one thing to offer him. How could I offer him anything when I wasn't there? A tie between us kept him there anyway. He attached himself to me with a fishing line from the shore and I reluctantly put up my hand and held on to it. I didn't move, but I did accept the connection and eventually he and I worked together, and I got out, but it took me a long time to dry off, and there were more waves to come.

Rowan had been sick for a few weeks before she told me she was pregnant and I and others had asked her if she could be pregnant, and she was insistent that this was not a possibility. I asked her one day, although I knew the answer, if she knew then that she could be pregnant and she said no, that she didn't believe she could be because she still couldn't believe what had happened to her. This confirmed what I had dreaded to hear. She had been raped. I knew it, I recognised it in the way she was, the words she used. Having a baby as a teenager, that's one thing I hadn't wished for my children, and being abused and raped was another. The hurt and sorrow for my child was incomprehensible, it still is.

CHAPTER TWENTY-NINE

In this mess Paul and I had agreed to move in together. He left his flat and moved into my new house. This was the worst time in the world to make this kind of decision but us being us we did it anyway. My soul spoke to me, but I didn't listen. Rowan moved in too, to this tiny house, and this was what we were doing. Rowan was having a baby, I would, because she comes before me, help her and support her and make it as lovely as having a baby should be, despite the circumstances. Florence was settling down a little after all the upheaval and having John in the house was a great help, and also, he was a lot of fun. Me being me thought to myself, perhaps this is ok, perhaps I have successfully held it all together, found a good partner and the kids are mostly intact. I used to call Paul my Paddington. Watching the film one day we were all there in the small sitting room, toys, and crafting materials all over the floor, eating snacks, and I remember feeling quite happy as I looked around. In the film Paddington comes in and causes a lot of chaos but in that he makes everything better and I thought to myself, this is Paul. Not that he had caused chaos as such, but he was so different. Loud, and funny and enthusiastic and a bit clumsy but yes, I thought, here is my Paddington.

When it transpired that Rowan was unhappy living with Paul and thought I had made a mistake moving in with him, tensions in the home rose. The thing that hit home as a painful truth was when she told me she did not want her child to form a relationship with Paul, because she was not overly confident in him being a permanent feature in her child's life. So, diplomatically, she told me she didn't place any blame on me, she understood why these changes had taken place, but the facts remained in her mind and experience that I was not reliable, not capable perhaps, of making secure and safe choices in partners and for that she had suffered. She was doing what she should, she should protect her child, but the pain this caused me to know that she had to protect her child against me was unbearable. I wanted to rip it off, to run away from it, to burn it, there wasn't one thing I wouldn't have done to get rid of that pain, but it stuck on.

I never tried to pretend that my life choices hadn't impacted my children, I knew that, but until then I thought that my love for them counted more. That I had been a good mother despite everything that was happening in our lives, that these other things affected us, but I protected them and kept them safe throughout it all. I was strong, I was the one who didn't cry and carried on for them.

There was no argument, there was nothing I could say to take this truth away, and like a child that day as she spoke, I sobbed, I wailed, my insides burned and there was nothing I could do to stop it. In all that I have written you might find it hard to believe but this was the most upset and confused I had ever felt in my life before. An example I guess of what I had been trying to say to Rowan. It isn't that you don't matter when you have a child, but you just no longer matter as much as your child. To say that guilt and regret filled up every part of my body and soul that day would be an understatement. I don't like uncertainty, I like resolution, and this was a situation I could not resolve, I could not put any of it back and repair the damage it had done, and now I had to pay the price. I had to reap what I had sowed but worse than this, so did the children. Brian's words rang through my head. In his many abusive messages to me he would say, you do this, you bring all of the shit upon yourself, now reap what you have sowed. All my life choices, I made them. My father said the same. You made your bed now lie in it. You decided to have babies with useless men and now you have no money and no life chances. Don't ask me for help, it is not here for you.

With my limbs and soul torn and pulled to pieces, I struggled to keep it all together over the next few months. I had to look in the mirror and see the truth. I had caused harm to my children. I thought I was good but in fact I was bad. Every negative thought I had about myself chimed up with a collective 'we were right about you'. Bad. Selfish. Weak. Stupid. Reckless. Wretched, putrid, ugly human. Die.

I started to take the good old antidepressants again. The ones that numb the emotions. They are the ones I needed to survive, and I started work with a psychotherapist next. It saved me really and started some of the actual healing I thought I had done before but hadn't even scratched the surface of. In all this we had covid and lockdown, my business going up the proverbial creek and the ever-rising tension between Paul and the girls. I was in no fit state to manage the relationship between he and I and neither was he. I drove out of the house one night with the intention of driving off a cliff. I'd been there before, and the feelings are real. I could not bear the pain but, as always, the children pulled me back. I would never in this world leave them as my parents had done to me.

Circumstances, practicalities and finances meant that Paul stayed at the house despite the tension and Rowan stayed too even though she didn't want to and after my beautiful grandson was born Rowan was even more fierce in her protection of both me and her son. When arguments happened between Paul and I she could not stay quiet and before my eyes the relationship, whatever that was at the time, shattered. Words were said, things were done that cut in those ways that a cup of tea and a 'I'm sorry about that' were not going to fix.

Paul eventually just had to leave despite him having nowhere to go, it was just impossible for him to stay, and I believe he never forgave me for this. The thing is, I would never have forgiven myself If I had put him before my child, not again and not after everything she had told me. Another huge overwhelming, cow dung sized pile of guilt landed in my body. I had hoped beyond hope that we could all sort things out and live happily. Paul was many things to me, but one was an enormous help in the home and with Florence, and I had begun, reluctantly, to rely on him. I hated myself for becoming so reliant on this man. I never did that, and this was why, now I had to manage alone again. Great fucking job Silvia you massive twat.

CHAPTER THIRTY

When I was talking to the psychotherapist, we worked through the arguments between Paul and I and Rowan. I remember she asked me what I thought I should do next. Did I think this was a good relationship? I said to her I just did not know.

"No," my soul said, "you do know."

I did too but I did not want to know and that is the difference. I knew that the facts told me this man should not be speaking to me the way he often did, that his words were abusive. If I went by the rules of what people say a relationship should be like, then this broke the rules. I said to her, I'm worried because I know I should feel something, but I don't. I miss him but it's causing such a lot of conflict in my mind because the rules say I should end this relationship. I had no faith in my ability to make decisions, you see, that was the real problem. What I wanted was for her to tell me what to do. I did not want to get it wrong, I wanted to get it right and be good.

All my life I strived to get it right and be good and the approval and acceptance of everyone and anyone, I might add, was so incredibly important to me, so why did I do the most insanely reckless and illogical things which were wrong? I use right and wrong here as words to illustrate my point but fully accept that the concept of right and wrong is questionable. Every time I thought I was on track, some stupid action would land me in yet another predicament. It was as if I just had to fuck it up and if I wasn't fucking it up who even was I?

She concluded that a likely or possible explanation – two words which for me meant chaos in my mind because these words are not conclusive – was that I had a borderline personality disorder. This sounded quite a plausible diagnosis, but I wasn't entirely convinced and needless to say neither was she, or at least she wasn't prepared to put her professional neck on the line and state it as fact. I examined the symptoms and signs of borderline personality disorder intensely, trying to identify myself in them.

Poor self-image – yes, that was true, I did.

Trouble directing themselves – whatever that means, but yes, I could say I lacked direction at times, unsure of where I was going or what I was supposed to be doing, so this sounded about right.

Impulsive and damaging behaviours – oh yes, well there it was, I could identify with this one very well. This must be it.

Intense and quickly changing moods – yes, I could agree, I mean, in one day I could go from ecstatic to devastated to suicidal and then forget all about it and sit laughing at a tv show that evening as if nothing had occurred, so yes, this one fitted well.

Feelings of emptiness – very often yes, but was that because I was empty? I felt very alone a lot of the time, but I was alone so I would, wouldn't I?

Paranoid thoughts when stressed – absolutely! Everyone hates me, my family are all going to die, my boyfriend is cheating on me, my boss thinks I am useless. Wow, yes, I could add this one for sure and I felt stressed a lot of the time.

Dissociated when stressed – if this means I struggle to speak, see, or feel at times, then yes.

Abdominal issues – my collection of stomach easing medicines, remedies and relieve IBS self-help books said yes to this one.

Unstable relationships – yes, just yes, I don't need to say any more.

Misinterpreting facial expressions – yes, I thought, I had never considered it before, but I always check this out, and am often unsure if I am reading it right, but is this trauma? Fear?

This therapist taught me some very helpful things. That a bad day didn't mean a bad month or several months. That I had a choice over what I wanted to pay attention to. The therapy I had done in the past had lifted large portions of the trauma energy but the real stuff, the stuff that made it possible to live life and not just muddle through hoping for the best, was and is harder to do. In my experience it is worth it because, for the majority of the time that is what I do. I do live. I am alive.

CHAPTER THIRTY-ONE

My youngest child, Florence, is also a formidable female. My uncle once said to me he was never in any doubt over the strength of women and their capabilities, having never come across anyone other than strong women in his family. My girls are a force, that's not a surprise.

From day one, Florence has been on the go, even as a newborn baby she rolled around her cot, restless, unable to sleep, and as soon as she was on her chubby little legs and could utter her first words, she was off. This sounds all so rosy and lovely, oh what fun, a busy chatty child full of creative energy. Yes, it was, and it is lovely, but also exhausting and I had postnatal depression and after the horrific pregnancy my body just really needed a rest. Not an afternoon, not an hour, a good long concentrated rest. I got no rest. Brian, despite promising to support with Florence's care, just wasn't there. I sat in disbelief at times. He looked at me, heard me say I had not slept and needed to sleep but yet he left us anyway. This was, as he consistently told me, to go to work, yes, I understood that, but on those days when he was not at work, he had the option to support me or to go to the pub and he always chose the pub. He left me, he abandoned me when I needed him, when I thought I had it right and yet again I had made a mistake. The lack of sleep I had and the hours it took night after night and then year after year, to settle this child to sleep was tantamount to torture, added to the triggering of my PTSD, ruined in a way what was supposed to be a wonderful time in my life. I think back to the conversations with Brian when he told me how surprised he was that I wanted to end our relationship, then I remember this and I think to myself, where were you? Anyway, it was one of those things that was in my life but became so normal that I became numb to it most of the time. When you have to carry on and there is no choice then you just do. I had been down that road before, that's for sure, I knew this game, I could play it well. No wonder it all came to a head, I think now, no bloody wonder I cracked.

I always said to people. Florence is so like me as a child, I remember doing these things myself. Sometimes it's as if I am watching myself, it's so strange, I would say. She would get it into her mind that she was going to do something. A back flip off the trampoline that she had just watched a kid do on YouTube. Off she would go and expect right there right now to be able to do it, and she would not stop despite this being kind of unrealistic. One day, yes, but that afternoon this was not going to be achieved. The frustration and the upset would ooze out of her, and we all felt it. I remember being the same. One day I decided I was going to build myself a Wendy house. I was so little I didn't have the strength to saw a piece of wood even but I carried on regardless, because to me this was a mere technicality and this isn't one of those stories where in the end I did make a Wendy house or she did spend the day practicing and the result was that she became the world's youngest gymnast to back flip twenty times off a back yard trampoline. No, I actually didn't know how to build a Wendy house and I couldn't do it but that hadn't stopped me trying, or indeed having 100% faith that this was going to work, and it never stopped her either. Yes, I berated myself because I couldn't and stamped on the bits of wood and threw the nails around. Yes, she screamed and stamped her feet and shouted at me to make her be able to do it and ended up in a teary mess on the sofa watching *Frozen* yet again while I wished for my eyes and ears to melt, but this is faith. This is a high level of optimism; is this verging on delusional or is it something else? Sleep. Yes, the sleep issue, I had that too. I understood her on this one, but it did not help.

When we all got locked in our homes in 2020 Florence was

seven, nearly eight years old. Not to mention the fact that overnight my business was obsolete as I could no longer see people face to face for their therapy sessions, the enormity of the LOCK IN, as I like to call it, illuminated our lives more than you could ever imagine. Stress levels were at their highest. This child did not fare well being locked in and being locked in with her was no fun for anyone. Then the home schooling started. I cannot describe the difficulty and frustration I felt even starting this process, which involved logging on to a school computer system which was unreliable and to me so ridiculously complicated. I was looking at the laptop, but I could not actually see. Very odd, very confusing. Then I had to somehow get this furious child, fizzing with energy, to do the schoolwork. The two of us together were like two negative magnets trying to touch, a literal cloud of unrestrained energy between us, and in the middle all reason, all understanding, all sanity, was completely lost. For a long while, too long, way longer than was necessary we, or rather *I*, soldiered on. It was what we were meant to do. Each miscommunication after the other built more and more tension, and it wasn't until we had a lull in the lock in and the children went back to school for a short time that I finally stopped and had a look around at what was going on. Things had deteriorated between Florence and I so much that I had enlisted the help of a parenting counsellor. I was out of my depth, so I also decided to ring her teacher because I had been wading through thick mud for so long it had become normal, then this unfamiliar situation came upon us and shone its light on every crack, and I had to ask for help. It pained me, it hurt me, but I had to. Asking for help or accepting help, to me, meant failure and it went back to when I very first became a mother, and the message was, 'your mess your problem,' and it went back to the relationships where every bit of help had to be repaid in some grotesque way, so asking for help did not naturally flow for me. This time, though, I was desperate enough to ask.

As so very often happens when change is on the way and is happening whether we like it or not, the school had that very day been talking of Jasmine. Their thoughts, she proceeded to tell me, were that Jasmine may have ADHD. I was less surprised than I thought I would be to hear these words. I knew this child was different. They are all 'different' though, aren't they? Different to my other two, that's for sure, but also, I knew her so well. It was as if she was different but the same. And when I say the same, I mean the same as me.

CHAPTER THIRTY-TWO

As the slow process of assessment for ADHD began for Florence, a rapid process of discovery began for me.

Symptoms of ADHD:

Difficulty focusing – well, it's taken me 6 years to write this book for one but, yes, I find it painful to focus at times. Let us look back to my life, especially at school. My mind was off on a wander as soon as my bum hit the seat and focusing on what the teacher was on about was near impossible. Focusing upon what people are saying in a conversation is really difficult too but before now I had not considered it to be anything other than the fact that I found what they were saying fairly uninteresting. What I realised is that I had unconsciously created all these coping mechanisms to keep myself engaged and focused when talking to someone. I repeat in my mind what they have said, I use sound. Yes, I see, mmm, hmmm and so on. I tell them openly I am not good at remembering names, dates and such like, I have found this is a socially acceptable downfall, so I have embraced it with a laugh, and it seems to appease them. I stop and write things down in my diary and again I make a joke about my memory being like a sieve. This has always been met with a nod of agreement about how they too also forget things from time to time. *From time to time* is the big difference here. When you have a neurotypical brain, you can forget things such a names or dates from time to time. When you have ADHD, you forget all of this information immediately every single time, unless you write it down or use some sort of other adaptation to preserve these details. None of these tactics are 100% reliable either, which makes for more stress. I have events written in my diary but if I don't open my diary or I do not know where my diary is, then that information is not available to me. Being a therapist is great because I can literally write down notes as the person speaks, which is not acceptable at the pub, but when I have my therapist hat on, I am fully engaged in the conversation. Why? Because the motivation is different, that's why. The motivation is that my brain is powered by my role, my responsibility, my values, my ethics are to give that person the attention they need or have indeed paid good money for. There is sadly less motivation to listen to a conversation in a café or at an event or a party, there just is. I was starting to understand why both myself and my family often accused me of being disengaged and disrespectful even when once again I forgot an important birthday or indeed, I may have remembered, I may even have bought the card and the present but the part where I needed to put that in the post was not completed. Despite all of my efforts, the most disconcerting thing is when you lose your mind, and it has taken a trip somewhere without you noticing, and then you do notice. Something like a direct question might bring it back – do you agree? – mate, I might or indeed I might not. Yes, I have been looking at you for the past 10 minutes, probably nodding my head, but I haven't one clue, not an inkling of what you just said. Now, apparently that's an ADHD symptom.

Difficulty regulating emotions – Yes, this was true, I did. I could, as I have said, have a whole medley of emotions in one day and when buttons were pressed, I almost watched myself react from afar. I saw it, I wanted to stop it, yet there I was reacting all over the place, emotions in disarray. I have worked the most on this particular issue without knowing what it was. It is a work in progress, but I am aware, and I can manage myself better if I haven't had alcohol. But what I know now is that if I drink alcohol when I am upset or I have something on my mind, it's not going to be a good move. Does my impulsivity kick in and say fuck it have the extra shot of tequila? Yes, it does my friends, yes it does. Do I then proceed to either cry myself to sleep or end up having an argument with my boyfriend over something I definitely can't remember saying or text my friend a long message about how sorry I am for being such a terrible person? Yes, yes, I do.

I do also know that taking care of my body, my soul, my emotions on a regular basis, helps. This is good motivation for my brain. I recently watched an interview with the television presenter Chris Packham, he was diagnosed as being autistic as an adult, but he was talking about his aversion to physical contact and how, as a famous person, people often came up to him and wanted to shake his hand or stand close to him while they got their picture taken with him. He was explaining that as a younger person he would not have been able to cope with the overwhelm and uncomfortable emotions that would evoke in him, but as he has matured, he has practiced managing this, and while he still dislikes these encounters where his space is invaded in a way he would not choose, he can manage it without going into a complete meltdown. I felt it was interesting because this illustrates that there are so many ways in which we have to train our minds to comply, but also that our brains can learn new ways of feeling and reacting that might be more beneficial for us. I wholeheartedly agreed with his aversion to strangers especially touching him. I found it physically painful as a child if someone were to hug me without me consenting, and for a long time, I would actively avoid situations where there might be the possibility of hugging, New Year parties being one for sure. I absolutely loved the no hugging rules in lock in, pressure off, happy days. Now I have taught myself that I can accept and manage a hug from a person I know, and I can even enjoy it and I read it does have benefits. It has to be on my terms and my soul must jump forward and practically stand in front of me if someone attempts to come near me for a hug and I don't want one, because I see them physically step back. They find it hard to look at me and shuffle away, and I think to myself, that's right, carry on by, nothing to hug here.

Impulsivity – this was the one that really helped me the most. Not that being impulsive is a good thing necessarily, I mean it's got me into a lot of hot water in my life, but knowing that impulsivity was part of ADHD, that helped. In my life it really has caused me quite a lot of unnecessary stress and regret and probably still will, but it explained something that bothered me so so much. Why? Why did you do that? It never made any sense to me; it never made any sense to anyone else, and then people were also angry at me while I was already angry with myself. This gave me peace to a certain degree, and awareness. Awareness is one of the greatest tools for recovery, for happiness for fulfilment, you name it, I believe it to be so greatly beneficial.

Difficulties with relationships – yup.

Poor self-image – yes again, I did have that, do have that sometimes still, and this is the painful knock-on effect of ADHD because all of this difference, which they call neurodiversity, makes you feel bad about yourself. Always in a state of confusion, missing key pointers throughout your day, this is not an easy place to be in and I just thought it was all me just being useless. The realisation that a large proportion of what had been happening in my mind was because I had ADHD, this awareness; well, it was just colossal.

Obsessing or hyper-focusing on some things – massive tick, just massive and if you think I let this revelation lie and did not spend my time researching and thinking and talking and writing about ADHD, what it means, what we can do about it, how it fits into my life, what it meant for Jasmine, for her life, worrying about how it might affect her life, obsessing about the possible dangers, the positives, joining groups, leaving groups that upset me, fighting for rights, for injustice against people with ADHD, and the list goes on and on, well I did not let it lie. The thing that really screwed with my head, which kept me awake for hours and hours obsessively trying to work it all out was what was real and what was me? What was trauma? If you looked up a list of symptoms that people who have suffered trauma experience the list would be very similar to symptoms of ADHD and BPD and I needed to resolve it. The cruel irony is that this is a very common result of having an ADHD brain. Things need to be finished, to be resolved with answers, this situation was full of unanswered questions, and I was in turmoil. My head became trapped in the process of remembering and putting pieces together. I could not stop, event after event fell into my mind.

I struggle to sleep at night, which is yet another contradiction because I can fall asleep anywhere and anytime during daylight hours. I once went out on a university night out and a student came up to me and said,

"Hi, you're that girl who falls asleep in every lecture," and she was not wrong.

I sat down and my eyes closed and at the end I woke up. I was even interested in the subject this time! Honestly, I think that as I have got older, I have just got more and more tired because it is overwhelmingly tiring living with trauma and having a brain that is not keen on shutting off. When I feel comfortable, I think my body says to itself, quick let her go to sleep right now because we don't know when we will get another opportunity, and so I do, I just fall asleep and that in itself can be a bit of an issue when I have shit to do or kids to look after. Like my own child, I hated going to sleep when I was little, but what's more, I hated the silence that it brought. Lights off and silence and feeling alone, and it wasn't as if I could just go to sleep and it would soon be morning, I could not sleep so being alone in bed was something I came to fear. When we moved to Newcastle and we stayed in the holiday house, there was a TV in my room. I slept with it humming away in the background and it helped. I remember the freedom I felt as I grew older and could have my records playing as I slept or the radio on in my room. I was never told to put them off by my mother, perhaps she knew. Now I sleep with music or a meditation on my phone. Silence is really hard for me. Silence is never silence and, in the silence, I feel alone but I can also hear things that others don't hear, and they get louder and louder and louder. In an attempt to look at my phone less, I got myself an alarm clock with a battery. I found it at a car boot sale, a seventies green retro-looking thing, and funnily enough I came across it recently whilst having a clear out. I had hidden it one night under all my winter jumpers in a drawer because the ticking had become unbearable to hear. This is ADHD. I felt alone and I felt different. This is because I was alone, and I was different. Even as a child I valued time alone because I wasn't getting in anyone's way or getting into trouble, so by default I was alone, and I got used to it. Being alone was free from pressure and free from criticism, but as ADHD very often does, the contradiction was that I wanted beyond anything else to be accepted and not alone, or at least not alone because people didn't like me. I began to be aware and to accept that I approached situations differently to others. Our family, whatever that may look like, is our main source of early learning and of value setting in our brains. I was segregated. The girls and Silvia. The one with the horrible father who was unkind, the one who wasn't as clever or talented as the girls. At school naturally because I wasn't listening in class for, I would say, 99% of the time, I wasn't able to complete the work, so I was different to the people sitting next to me because they were able to do it, they had been listening. This is really where the thing they refer to as masking started for me. I wasn't actually stupid I just hadn't been listening! I didn't know this at the time, so to cover up my huge lack of ability at school I rejected school and fully embraced being naughty. Like all best laid plans this had flaws and big gaping holes in it, but nonetheless the plan was in motion, and so I didn't go to school and gave zero fucks for the consequences because, well, I am impulsive like that. Hello again ADHD. As a child I couldn't sit still, despite having a great big, massive hole in the centre of my heart that was leaking blood throughout my body, I got up and ran around anyway. As I have got older the restlessness has gone inside. I have learned that getting up and running around is not acceptable in most social or working situations, so the energy has gone inside. I didn't realise that the way I constantly bite the inside of my mouth and tap my fingers is all a way for my body to let that energy run. I have clear memories of sitting in situations with family, with friends or lots of people around me and being very unsure of what was being said because I couldn't follow the conversation. I felt stupid and I went inside. I used to think I was shy, but in actual fact I just found it really confusing to be with lots of people and to join in, not because I was shy but because I hadn't a clue what had just been said. This had to have been the ADHD. I'd try to join in and usually something unrelated or inappropriate would come out, and I felt embarrassed and then I was shy, and my self-esteem did shrink. I wanted to join in, but I felt exposed, so I went inside, and as I have got older that has had a huge impact upon my life. Making friends, but more importantly keeping friends, has been excruciating at times. Yet again it brings me back to why it has been easier for so many reasons to stay alone. One day I decided I would go to university, so I did, and this is a great example of why I have a lot of fondness and respect for my impulsivity, but I looked on at everyone else making these lifelong university friends and was resolute in my belief that this simply was not for me. My masking guardian kicked in and the narrative became, I don't really like people, I am not really a people person, I prefer to be alone. Then I'd go on a uni night out, get really drunk and make a massive twat of myself and want to die… again.

When I got my job as a social worker, and I had some really serious responsibilities, I put a lot of this down to stress. I was stressed and that did not help, I also had PTSD, that didn't help either, but when I wrote a meeting with no time or location in my diary, or I was late to a meeting because, despite having driven to the destination several times before, I just could not find it and then took for what seemed like a thousand years to decide upon which parking space to use, I'd decided that this was just stress. Apparently not, this is essentially severe ADHD symptoms. Numbers are an enigma to me. I'm telling you, I don't know any of my times tables, and if people suggest I learn them, as they have done over the years, I feel a rage towards them that I know I shouldn't. I've felt rage towards my kids for asking me to help them with their maths homework even, and that rage very quickly turns to the teacher, to the system, to the whole world for even suggesting that I, on this previously calm and pleasant evening, should have my brain opened up to the hell that is 8x7 when I hadn't been asking for it. I live my life now the way I like it and this entity called maths homework has come in here with no right and ruined it all. As a social worker, I very often had to get money for people, use money for outings and the like. In a government institution, this meant filling in forms about money and money is all about numbers. I kid you not, in the 10 years that I worked as a social worker I used my skill and creativity to wangle my way out of ever filling in any of these straight from actual hell forms, because quite simply I couldn't, and if that meant putting all my energy that day into getting someone else to do it for me then I was prepared to put that work in. That, I have discovered, is ADHD and I feel better about myself with this information.

Depression effects motivation. Depressed people struggle to motivate themselves, to eat well perhaps, or to go outside, to clean their home or clean themselves. The things that have happened to me in my life have unquestionably accrued levels of depression and I have felt this deep sense of lifelessness, where I have no inclination to do anything. As I started to recover from the life events and my depression lifted, I still felt these waves of tiredness and lack of motivation. I would look and look at piles of washing and the thought of putting them away made me want to cry but then later that day I would be ok getting on with something else. As my knowledge about ADHD continued, this became more and more apparent. This wasn't depression, this was ADHD.

These questions wouldn't go away. Am I still me? If I did these things because of my ADHD, where am I? It's not like I was under the influence of a magical drug, and it made me do all these things and think all of these things and now I am on a come down. It's still there because ADHD is not something I can recover from and heal from. This was it, the part that really got to me. In my life so far, I had experienced an unfortunate event and recovered from it, or I had become depressed, and I had recovered, or I had anxiety and then I did things and my anxiety subsided. Up until this point the depression and anxiety had loomed there in the background. Recovery is a long process, getting rid of some of the shit on my stick that has happened to me, is almost like it has been writing this book, a life's work. Finding out I had ADHD was something I could recover from, but I couldn't actually recover from ADHD. I went into a whole lot of catastrophising with this one.

I will never ever have the tidy home to which I aspire so much. I love it when my house is tidy, and I thought that when I was 'better' my house would be tidy all the time. I will never get rid of this underlying anxiety exacerbated by my constant feeling of inadequacy and disappointment to others. I thought the fact that going food shopping made me want to cry, die or starve was something that I would eventually get over. I thought that, eventually, I would have my act together and no longer fuck up my child's life by making poor life decisions, forgetting they have a school trip or school photographs, or they are off to a party and need a gift and a card for that child, or they need money for something, or my own *purse* when we have driven 50 miles to a theme park for the day, or to buy milk again (and there is also no bread), or not have the mental and physical capacity to play with them or speak to them because I just need to sleep right now, or remember what it is that they like to eat or do or what they wanted for Christmas, to not lose focus when they are talking to me and for them to think I don't care about them, to stop doing random things like suddenly deciding to move house or move their school to counteract some other disaster going on in our lives, to stop acting like a gabbling buffoon in front of their friends, or worse their friends' mothers, to stop putting us in regular financial jeopardy each time I sprout a brand new business idea. As I write this my belief in myself and eternal optimism scoff as my brain says to me that all my business ideas are absolutely bound to work out, and here it is. Back around to what is me and what is the ADHD. And if it's the ADHD and I have no control, then holy fuck, will I survive the next 40 years now that I've decided to stay on this rollercoaster after all?

CONCLUSION

I love a conclusion, and I love one so much that I have named this chapter *The Conclusion*! but the truth is there is never going to be a firm conclusion to my life, and I am never going to get all the answers and conclusions that I seek, so for my own mind's sake let's call this a pause. A pause where I can take stock, reflect and prepare for the next part of my life, and this seems a good a place as any. It is as if my life allowed me a pause to finish this book at a point where it all changed again.

Your life can change in a moment. This sounds like the strap line for a Tony Robbins seminar (other inspirational life coaches are available), I know, but it is true. You move house from the countryside to the town. Your life changes in a moment. Your mother dies. Life changes from the moment it happens. You get raped. Life changes. You have a child. One moment you are not a mother, the next you are, life changes. Your father kills himself, you meet a new person, you walk to the shop, you don't walk the shop, you take the job, you don't, you book the holiday, you end the relationship, you do not. Each moment there is the unstoppable force that is change. What I discovered is that we are in control over a lot more of that change than I had originally thought. Co-creation exists, and we are doing it all the time. I realised that in a moment and while I might not have put it into conscious practice straight away, it changed the way I viewed life. That's a momentous start.

This is not the part where I tell you the secret to a life of your dreams. I don't have a £100,000 programme that I can sell you that will teach you how to manifest your way to a perfect life just like mine in three easy steps. I have impulsively purchased way too many of those programmes than I am ever prepared to admit, and the only easy part is putting in your bank details. How do they know what my perfect life is like anyway?

I want to live my life and be happy with the way I live it. That is not to be mistaken for a wish for a happy life. These two things are quite different. Living a life in a way that you are happy with can bring great peace for your soul.

I was never in a million years going to able to come to this conclusion when my life was in such disarray and chaos for so many years. A thing that I find fascinating is that for my whole life people have said to me that I am so very calm, and I often think if only you knew what I was facing at home today or what is actually going on inside my body right now. My children will probably disagree, my partners over the years, yes, they have seen me lose my shit many times, but I tell you, I have never done this lightly. What I know about myself is that when I lose my shit, I need to act because I am not ok, because I value calm and peace so very highly. That's me, and that isn't the ADHD. I recognise that being calm and grounded is a way to survive almost any situation, perhaps any situation, so now in my life I work not on recovering but on keeping my body and my mind and my soul calm and grounded. Preferably lying under a tree in a pine wood smelling the sweet aroma of the air filled with moss and damp bark, or with my body immersed in the sea, the cold water pinching my skin and telling me we are alive. Failing that, when I am doing the grocery shopping at the supermarket or sitting on my sofa with a cup of coffee procrastinating about washing the dishes, a feeling of calm right there in my body is of highest priority in my life. When I feel it, the gratitude I can muster is tremendous.

The therapy I have done so far, the counselling, the hypnotherapy, the psychotherapy, the medication even, has been the start. I was able to consider how our emotions are stored in our cells and understand that it was emotion causing the real chaos to my cells, this learning was vital, but then what. I had to learn to live with what was left and that was me, ADHD and all, and it is never going away because it is me. I thought to myself, I could sit here for a year and a day figuring out why and what and how but what ifs are the road to nowhere good. I think we need to do it though. We need to be in a place where we ask the questions and feel the emotions about what has happened to us. It is part of the process, as they say. To quote a favourite movie line of mine:

"They say a lot, don't they?" (*Pulp Fiction*)

Whether it is ADHD-related or not, I had to do that for a while at least. Its unkind to ourselves at times, it really hurts our very core but if we don't look at it all it just stays inside festering away and then eventually it erupts and there is no going back. Perhaps it all just happens when it's meant to happen, and we do what we need to do at the time. I have read enough books about the mind, the brain, the universe, to know there are no clear answers to this stuff, and I certainly don't have them. I want to be honest about that. My story is what happened to me and how I survived, which I did. How I did that takes us back to the questions and the need for answers.

I remember I was at a friend's house and a lady there was telling us about this book she had read called *The Secret*. If you haven't read this book, it professes to tell you the secret path to all health, wealth and happiness, generally speaking. First off, this shouldn't be a secret, this isn't a secret, and it also isn't the answer all wrapped up in one tidy book, in my opinion. At the time, as I learned about the universal law of attraction which, again, isn't a secret, I was aggrieved. The way I heard it in my body of pain and trauma, was that all the pain I had gone through was essentially my own doing. My vibe was low and negative, and therefore all this negativity, pain and sorrow had attracted itself to me. When Brian left, full of anger towards me, he told me that I reaped what I sewed, I would be unhappy, and it was only what I deserved. I sat with these words, they played into every bad thing I had ever been told about myself and felt about myself. I was bad and therefore I got what I deserved.

How do you turn that around, how do you stop thinking so badly about yourself? Time, effort, awareness, kindness and forgiveness. These things have been key. It takes time to retrain your brain. Time, but also experience, which sadly rarely comes without time having passed. Youth is wasted on the young, as my grandmother would say. Now that time has passed, I can look back to see all of those situations for what they were. Things that happened to me, choices I made, mistakes, achievements and everything in-between. The certainty of the past is that it cannot be changed. I didn't want to sit there anymore in that pain, and that was a conscious decision I made using everything the past had taught me. My experiences all taught me something, but they were not punishments for my negative vibe or my low vibration.

I read a book by Carolyn Myss called *Anatomy of the Spirit*. I'm reluctant to say that it changed my life as that seems a tad extreme but while this book itself perhaps did not change my life, it was certainly part of a catalyst that did. What I heard from this book, in no uncertain terms, was that I had to take control of my spirit, my soul, my very being. Silvia, who was lost, smashed to pieces all over the place, I had to gather her up and pull her back together. What she really opened my eyes to was the concept of living consciously. That sodden coat, so heavy on my back, was not allowing me to live consciously. It was keeping me right where my subconscious mind liked, in the familiar uncomfortable past and this is where the awareness comes in. Awareness is a far more constructive way to view events in your life than guilt. It definitely takes the edge off, I can tell you. I am aware of the mistakes I have made, and I am aware of why they happened, how they happened and everything that happened as a consequence, but I had to forgive myself. Awareness of ADHD helped me to do that because a lot of the berating I gave myself was for things that happened because of the ADHD. That doesn't make it acceptable, far from it, but it is a cause, and this has helped me to forgive myself and dry off that part of the coat. Awareness of how the brain works under threat, what it can make you do, how it can distort things and how it can affect your ability to make decisions, that helped me. It also helped me to forgive others. Caroline taught me that in order to keep my own spirit intact I had to forgive others, it was essential in fact, because any energy I gave to not forgiving another person or a situation took power and energy away from me and I needed, still need, all my pieces intact and with me not somewhere else wasting time on things that have passed and gone. In the numerous texts by Caroline Myss I have now read, book upon book has spoken to me and opened up even just the idea that there are other ways of living and feeling. My ADHD made it extremely difficult for me to read long texts, much to the disgust of my parents who each night scoffed at me for not sitting in bed reading like the rest of the family, but now I know this about my brain I have discovered audiobooks and it's been a true gift. And in that gift, I have steadily worked my way through a catalogue of self-discovery titles by authors and teachers such as Deepak Chopra, Sophie Bashford, Jack Kornfield, Seth Godin, Napoleon Hill, Ram Dass, Will Smith, no less, the list could go on, and it will. There is always more awareness to be had. I think that being more in tune with my body and aware or more conscious, whatever you want to call it, leaves me nowhere to go except back to myself and what I need to do.

Kindness. How kind can you be to yourself? You often see this slogan written on a card or a reusable shopping bag. Ok, if you say so. Kindness comes in so many forms. Forgiveness, that's a form of kindness. Allowing yourself to learn and make mistakes, that's kindness. Taking time to heal, that's kindness. Making the effort to be well, that's kindness and this goes on because there are days, and I am quite sure there will still be days when I get up and I am angry at the world. I am angry at a person, and I allow my spirit to use up all that energy being angry and upset. There are often days when I look in the mirror and tell myself I look awful, and I feel hurt inside. There are days when I feel I am a bad mother, a bad friend, a bad businesswoman, a bad writer, a bad therapist, a bad partner, a bad sister, a bad everything some days. And you know what, maybe on those days I was being a bit of a crappy mother, maybe I shouted at my child when I shouldn't have or maybe I did forget it was school photo day again and I upset her. Maybe I wasn't doing what I needed to do in my business or producing writing that I was happy with. Maybe I did look a bit rough this morning and all of that is acceptable on some days and at some times. In my book it is anyway. I am not now professing to be a guru of perfected awareness and tranquillity sitting in a healed castle of divine insight. Despite my eternal optimism, I believe that a constant feeling of bliss is unachievable, but when we have a choice, which we do, it seems far better to send our energy into the things that help, rather than the things that don't.

This is the thing that I have really learned. Looking back on my life and the things that have happened, at the time a lot of them were out of my control, and by this I don't mean that I was a victim and that all of this stuff was done to me, and I hold no responsibility for any of it. No. I was responsible, of course I was. My trauma. My ADHD. My naivety. My youth. My lack of understanding or awareness. These things are all part of me, so by default of course I hold responsibility for all that has happened in my life. I used to think this was a bad and scary concept, but if we have the power and we have always had the power, then how wonderful. If I have the power over my own spirit then I will always be able to find a place of peace, calm, safety, and abundance. Somehow, I will.

In this I have released with purpose the concept of fault and in turn blame. Is it my fault that these things happened, did I indeed reap what I sowed, and did I deserve it all because it was my responsibility? No, of course not. If it's not my fault, is it my mother's, or my father's? Is it the teachers at school, the girls in my class? Is it my ADHD's fault? Is it the fault of the people who have abused me? Is it my sister's fault? No, I really do not think so, because with fault you inevitably get blame. With blame you get anger and with anger you plop yourself right back in the uncomfortable albeit familiar past where you are not really living. To truly move away and start living I have to see my life differently. I need to view every situation and every decision as the learning experience that it actually is. I do not in any way believe that in order to feel gratitude or empathy for others you need to have gone through suffering, but I did, and that is a valuable commodity that I possess.

In writing all of this, I am conscious that it could sound

idealistic, and to be honest if I'd read some of this while in any of those negative situations, I know, 100 percent, that I would have thought to myself, smug bitch. Think it's that easy, do you? Pop your positivity pants on and life's a peach, eh? Grab your 'Be Kind' shopping bag and float down to the woods to sit with the trees and all your cares will drift up to the sky like magical sunbeams. I get it. Here's the alternative, and I didn't read any of those books to work this part out. The alternative is that I sit in the biggest pity party full of sadness and upset and resentment you can imagine, drinking myself to destruction, living no life at all, hating everyone for all their smug happiness, and in that place you cannot see the beauty and the joy in anything, even time with your own beautiful children, and I know that because I've sat there a few times and it's really, really shit.

Sometimes there are big fat sit up and listen moments from your soul and sometimes these moments are more subtle. I say soul, because for me that's the part of you that really gives you the messages, even if it's that there are no messages, and it's so very tired and shrivelled that it's just sitting there, so lifeless. The more you listen to your body and the messages it tells you, the more your true intuition kicks in. When you say you don't know, you do, you just don't want to listen. When I talk about not listening to my soul, this is what I mean. You ask yourself a question and your soul answers, but you don't want to do it, and this has been true for me so many times. The relationship that makes you unhappy and you say to yourself, I don't know what to do. You do. Ending a relationship, no matter how sad it makes you, is a challenging and painful process. Untangling your life from another human is not an easy task, so we sit in that place where we claim we don't know what to do. This is what happened between and me. Yes, there were so many positives about our relationship, but it was pain that brought us together and pain that kept us together. When he left, we stayed in a relationship, and both claimed we were content with the situation, but his pain and my pain clashed. My optimism and faith in humanity, which I am so pleased has not ever left me despite my negative encounters with people, led me to ignore the flaws in our relationship. I made excuses and my soul tried to make me listen. I wanted more than anything for it to work but each move ended in more hurt. If I spoke about the issues, he closed me down, if I voiced my distress, he accused me of rocking the boat. Each action brought more discord and never the resolution I had been hoping for. I expected, given he was professing to be my life partner who loved each bone in my body and each part of my soul, that he would react to my distress with understanding and with love and compassion, and, yes, change his behaviour towards me. It's ironic that it was Paul who always said that expectation leads to disappointment. This was lovely when we were travelling around Europe with no kids in tow and we were free to expect nothing around the corner, and consequently each beautiful village that we encountered was a joyous revelation. The one time we expected the hotel we had booked to have mountain views and in fact they were views of a massive Sports Direct, we laughed about how true this law of the universe was. I was losing myself again. I was living my life in the shadow of what another person may or may not do. This was not on Paul; this was on me. I heard my soul telling me this wasn't right, and I felt it writhe in pain once again. My body was in pain, right inside my gut, it was a physical pain but after all the 'work' I had done, it made me embarrassed almost that I wasn't putting this awareness I now had into practice in this situation. As excruciating as it was, I could no longer ignore myself and I had to end the relationship, I just had to. I pulled in every excuse to keep it going. He is good with the kids, and he was, he was a brilliant person to have around when he was on top form. My Paddington, except on occasion he was actually really awful to them, and besides, he had left them too, as they had him in their lives and now he was absent, so, no, that was not enough. We have had such a lot of fun times together. Yes, we had, but also some really unpredictable awful ones that took me months to recover from, so, no, that's not enough, and of late I was finding it very difficult to recall a fun time we had experienced in each other's company. He is hurting too and full of trauma also, I know this is a factor in the way he responds to me. This was a big one because I knew it to be true, but was I actually saying to myself that his needs were greater than mine? His actions against me on occasion were so out of order and was I to sacrifice my own soul for his? Was I bad if I did this, was I being good? These questions caused turbulence to my already stressed and traumatised mind. There were no clear answers except from my soul, who simply told me, using the physical pain in my body, that this was no longer a safe and happy place for me, and I was to get out. I really did want to just run away, but of course unless I was going to leave my body and my soul behind, this was not going to resolve the situation.

On the day that I returned the small number of belongings he had left in my home, I cried. Hysterical loud crying, wailing almost. My inner child was stamping her feet, saying but I wanted this to work! I thought you were a good fit, I thought you were going to love me and never leave me. You said that to me and now I want to know why this isn't working. I don't want to be alone; I don't want to start again and go through another relationship. I want, I want, I want! Paul poked his head through the open car window on the passenger side and just before he left, he said to me,

> "Can I just give you one bit of advice before I go? Try and be a bit more satisfied with what you have in life, stop always looking for something."

Just like that, my tears stopped, and it was as if time paused for a moment. My soul turned to my child self and looked at her crying on the ground, feet crumpled on the floor, eyes puffy and red, cheeks stinging from the salt in the tears and sadness and desperation seeping out of every pore, and she said to her, get up Silvia. Get up right now. We will never settle for a life less than what we want or need again, now get up, wipe your tears, it's time to go.

THE END

I believe this to be true. There is always some light to be seen in any dark situation. It might be really small and almost covered by the dark, but it is always there. The dark that surrounded my life made it very hard to see it for a while, that is also true. But looking back, the way you inevitably do when you write a book about your life, the light parts are so clearly evident. They show up even more. The moments of true gratitude, the moments when the angels arrived, the moments when I gathered myself and I got up, and despite feeling like giving up, I never did. I wouldn't be writing this if I had.

We all have the chance to tell our story in any way we choose. Not just in a book about your life but each and every day to yourself. You're the most important person to share anything with on a regular basis! You could say that the story you have just read is about a woman who lived a lifetime of being abused and used and of never fitting in. Tragedy filled every corner of her world. Each time she tried to move forward yet another obstacle fell in her way, or she put one there herself. This woman made mistake after mistake. She let her family down, her children down and she never managed to secure or at least keep any of the things that were expected of her.

You could say that but, honestly, would you want this to be the story people tell about you? The sermon at your funeral filled with this drudgery? Fuck that. Try this instead.

There was a woman who as a small child learned of the beauty and power of the earth. The smell of the fresh clean air, the touch of the wildflowers, the cleansing power of the Scottish waters, it seeped into her soul. Her soul learned then that freedom was essential to her very being. After learning this she began training for the warrior woman she would become. Adversity taught her gratitude, empathy, strength, compassion and kindness. The adversity solidified her belief that she could do anything she chose. It confirmed to her that light exists, and that she could find it. She brought into the world three children. The oldest child, her only son, is well liked, respected, kind and tough. He does no harm to others and feels a sense of gratitude for what he has that others with more do not share. He is safe. He is happy. He is her beautiful boy who she loves so deeply that she cannot put it into words. The middle child, her oldest daughter, a powerful courageous mother herself now, who will never be told she cannot do anything. She can do it all and she does, and she will continue. She has wisdom beyond her years and she and the woman nurture each other and support each other. The woman is unsure how she would manage without this wondrous child. What a gift! The youngest child has brilliance. She is still so very young, but she makes sure she is heard. That is a good thing. The woman and this youngest child live together just the two of them in a house that looks onto fields and where the fresh air and the freedom are close. This fiery child is often a mirror of the woman. The likeness frightens her at times. She has to remember, and never forget, how it felt to be this child. As if there weren't enough blessing in this woman's life, she has another glorious child to love. Her grandson. The energy of this child is so abundant it almost hurts the woman's heart, it makes it swell so much. He is loved and wanted and safe.

The woman uses all her learnings to better support herself, her family and her business. Each time she meets a person she treats them with respect and offers as little judgment as she can because her soul remembers how it feels to be disrespected, shamed and criticised. She follows the direction of things that bring her fulfilment, that make her feel energised and safe. She consciously makes steps to walk away from negativity and resistance. She accepts herself, shadow and light. The dark bits are almost essential at times because they hold so many rich lessons. She realised the true essence of being the cocreator of her life and that is powerful. She is not just a bystander, letting people and situations and old beliefs dictate the course of events. She learned that accepting herself and offering herself true love brought her many more benefits than waiting for the acceptance and love of others. As scared as she was, she decided that being alone and not allowing herself to be supported was self-harm to the highest degree, so she smashed down the walls around her and threw the sodden coat in the bin. She grabbed her shitty stick, wiped it clean and used it as a fucking wand. A flood of joyful experiences washed up at her door and phenomenal people began to cascade into her life at an incredible rate. She lived her life by her own rules, and it felt *good*.

She and her soul had a serious talk.

"Soul?" she said.

"Yes?" said her soul.

"It took us a long time to get here, didn't it?"

"It sure did" her soul agreed, raising more than an eyebrow, "getting up has not been an easy road."

"I'm often still tired by this enormous journey," she

said.

"I know," said her soul, "me too, but now we are allowed to rest if we want to."

"Yes," said the woman, "I love that."

Her soul, it said to her, "You know, now that we have made it, I see no reason to ever go back down, do you? Shall we stay here?"

"Oh yes," replied the woman, as she sat with an abundance of beautiful gratitude and love within her body, "its wonderful up here and I feel that there is much more fun to be had than before."

"Absolutely!" said her soul, "much more fun for sure".

"What about music and dancing?" asked the woman.

"Without a doubt," replied her soul, "there will be endless opportunities for that, and we shall sing."

So, the woman and her soul made the decision to do everything within their power each and every day to stay up, and even when they felt like falling, and even when they fell, they worked together and found a way to get up again.

And that, dear reader, is also the truth.

GET UP

GET UP

GET UP

GET UP

GET UP

GET UP

GET UP

GET UP

Printed in Great Britain
by Amazon